Robert Chambers

HOW TO WRITE
PARODIES
AND BECOME
IMMORTAL

Library of Congress Cataloging-in-Publication Data
Chambers, Robert
How to Write Parodies and Become Immortal/Robert Chambers
ISBN-13: 978-1468139600
ISBN: 1468139606

Copyright © Robert Chambers, 2012
All Rights Reserved
www.parodybychambers.com

Library of Congress Control Number: 2011963656
CreateSpace, North Charleston, SC

To M. A. C. Again

Thank you.

Contents

Introduction

This book is a wholly undignified, nonacademic sequel to *Parody: The Art That Plays With Art* (Peter Lang Publishing, 2010), a scholarly attempt to set a very twisted historical record straight. In that work, I maintain that, contrary to hundreds of years of blather by experts, parody is not a trivial genre or type of writing, but is, instead, a transformative technique, accessible even to young children, that is chiefly responsible for innovation and change in *all* the arts. Parodists, in the course of their aesthetic travels, have created a large number of brand-new genres, including the modern novel, along with a very big pile of artistic masterpieces.

I can't write a masterpiece, and I can't teach you how to create one yourself. But I can show you, based on my ideas about the parodic technique, how to write a few parodies—mostly what I call "general parody spoofs," the variety of parody that typically appears in magazines that still print dribs and drabs of fiction.

I had originally tried to offer some of this instruction in *Parody: The Art That Plays With Art*. But my editor maintained that this kind of vo-tech material, which included my own parodies as examples, had no place in a scholarly work. He persisted in this position even though I had anticipated it and countered it with some observations by a very distinguished professor, Wayne C. Booth, late of the University of Chicago English Department.

In an essay entitled "How [Theorist Mikhail] Bakhtin Woke Me Up," Booth maintains that Aristotle, in his *Poetics*—the first great work of literary theory—not only describes tragedy, but also provides lots of implicit tips for actually creating tragedies. Instructing artistic folks, according to Booth, has been an ideal espoused by Aristotelian critics ever since. And Booth should know: all the members of his Chicago department once fed on Aristotle as single-mindedly as the tapeworms that dine upon the citizens of South Carolina.

So, in honor of Aristotle and in an act of homage to the Parodic Muse (a forgotten tenth daughter of Zeus and Mnemosyne named Lula), I am offering some practical advice while knowing full well that the initial mechanical simplicity of parody is partially responsible for its lowly reputation.

That deceptive initial simplicity has fostered a disconnect: not many Big-Time Tastemakers have perceived that simple parodic ingredients and mixtures can remain simple or be mustered to concoct labyrinths—to stay in the parodic nursery or to suddenly produce confounding new worlds. Parody, wrongly, is thought by most authorities to be elementary and unworthy stuff.

Further, those who write about the arts do not generally resemble Prof. Booth's helpful Aristotelian advisors. Instead, scholars and critics typically shun practical step-by-step tips about artistic construction and carpentry because such guidance is far removed from their career-oriented need to serve up peacock displays of intellectual virtuosity. For this reason, among others, in the world of Big-Time Tastemakers how-to instructions about cooking up works of art are accorded about as much respect as that granted to the metaphysics of flatulence.

I am at best a low-church Aristotelian who lives in craven fear of Big-Time Tastemakers, but I decided to forge ahead with this how-to book both because of my respect for Prof. Booth and my faith in what I call the "Butz Rule." It was devised by Earl Butz, sage Secretary of Agriculture in the Age of Nixon. Formally, his dictum can be stated this way: those who make or interpret the rules of a game (parody, in my case) should also play the game. Butz actually stated his mandate informally and more memorably than I have. As reported by *Time* on December 9, 1974, during that year's World Food Conference in Rome, Butz promulgated the rule in support of his call for birth control. A reporter had objected that the pope banned such practices. According to *Time*, Butz defended "his position in a mock Italian accent: 'He no playa the game, he no maka the rules.'"

In part, I tried to inject my own parodies into my earlier volume and now this one because I'm an egomaniac and long to see my work reprinted (in a few cases) or published for the first time. Further, I'm lazy: obtaining permission from publishers to reprint long passages or short works by their authors is often expensive, and, to my great surprise, I've learned that, despite the PR value in having a book mentioned or excerpted by others, many publishers seem to treat permission-seekers like computer viruses and throw up all manner of firewalls and other obstacles in the way of granting rights to their material (no wonder the publishing industry is dying). On the other hand, my own published stuff came easily—my parodies were printed in defunct magazines and two pieces appeared, without copyright, when I worked at *The Atlanta Journal-Constitution*.

Further, I have decided to take advantage of the outrageous fees accompanying permissions: I am going to charge myself ten thousand dollars for each of my stories printed or reprinted here. Thus, I will make 130,000 dollars even if no one even bothers to take a peek at this book. I could have charged myself more, of course, but there's no point in being greedy.

I am also including my work to prove that if I can write parodies, anyone can, and if I can get some of my work published, so can you, unless your imagination is wholly given over to visions of defecating mice.

Most of my parodies were written long ago, from the late 1970s through the 1990s. I cannot explain why I stopped writing them, but it's surely not because I've lost interest in the subject. The best explanation I can offer is that all my spare time in the last couple of decades has been devoted to growing yams and to conversing with these fascinating tubers in an attempt "to become one with nature." I think; therefore I yam.

A word of warning: serious, high-art parodies do not have to be funny (or even to be varieties of comedy, broadly defined—there are, for instance, works of tragic or sacred parody). But the kinds of simple parodies, mostly spoofs, that I will attempt to show you how to create are far from sacred or tragic.

I'm afraid, finally, that some of my parodies, because of their age, have become dated. I persist in offering them because they are still very fresh in terms of their dynamics and my understanding of them, meaning that these works still enable me to instruct you to the best of my abilities. And, believe me, my approach to the subject of parody is an unusual one. I cannot, of course, hope to compete with Aristotle. Sadly, his theoretical work on comedy and the instructions it may have contained have been lost for many hundreds of years. Here the best I can offer is sour grapes: maybe Aristotle wasn't much of a parodist or even a passably competent gag man.

Again, I dabbled in the creation of parodies during much of my youth, but my very modest success in publishing them occurred mostly in a brief three-year span (1978-1981). After that, I declared myself a victor and stopped collecting rejection slips. The following are my parodies that somehow made their way into print:

"The Grand Ole Chinoiserie Newsletter" was published in the April 1978 issue of *Off P'tree* magazine, pages 40-41.

"Hunger in Hungary" was published in the April 1979 issue of *Peachtree* magazine (the successor to *Off P'tree*) as "When You're Strictly from Hungary, Thought For Food's Food For Thought," by "Rob Willie," on pages 35-36. (I wrote a personal finance column in the same issue of the magazine, page 44, and the editor thought it wouldn't be seemly to have the author also identified as the fabricator of a bizarre little parody.)

"Whipping History" was published in the Sunday, November 30, 1980, *Atlanta Journal-Constitution* as "Out of the West Rides Cowboy Ron," on page 1D.

"Market Zen" was published on page 8B in the January 12, 1981, *Atlanta Journal* in a slightly different form as "Nonsense Is Sometimes Name of Stock Market Game" in my weekly column devoted to investigative snippets, business gossip, and financial trivia.

1.

Parodies Regained, An Overview

Warning: This chapter is atypically serious (compared to all the others), and if that sort of thing grates on your high-strung aristocratic temperament or your day-to-day flirtation with barbarism, I think you can get what you'll need just by studying the diagrams and the pictures. You will, of course, have to provide your own spit cup.

Confession time: I can teach you something about writing parodies, but only in a very limited way can I help you become immortal. My "immortality" promise is what is known in philosophical circles as "a cheap come-on." But I'm not being entirely accurate here: you can tear off your own chunk of permanence through the "Art Dream" that is so beautifully described by the warm-hearted old newspaper editor, Shrike, in Nathanael West's novel, *Miss Lonelyhearts*. Ultimately, your achievement of immortality will stem from publishing or self-publishing your very own parody or collection of parodies and then copyrighting and registering that material with the Library of Congress. There, as glorious and immutable Art, your masterpiece will reside forever and ever, or until a Bolivian terrorist in 2022 buys a nuclear device on the Internet for $49.95 and blows up Washington, D.C.

This chapter will begin explaining, a bit indirectly, I will admit, the process of creating parodies. With luck that information will emerge as I summarize my highly unorthodox understanding of this subject and my cruel mistreatment by the American Kennel Club.

It should soon be clear that, while parody can quickly become complicated, parody manufacturing begins with a simple set of maneuvers, an activity that almost everyone is equipped to perform. In fact, I believe most people were active parodists in early childhood.

So…you're just out of practice.

To get you back up to speed, I've tried to boil down and simplify the material and the ideas in my academic study, *Parody: The Art That Plays With Art*. The upcoming relatively painless dose of gibble-gabble will permit you to ease into the complex areas of the subject with a high level of understanding—and will introduce the tools you'll need for getting underway.

Contrary to hundreds of years of commentary by experts, and distinct from what nearly every dictionary, handbook, or full-scale work will offer as a definition, parody is not a trivial genre, or type of writing, nor is it simply a collection of equally minor little genres. Parody is, instead, a supremely important technique that generates disparate contrasts and that is applicable to all varieties of communication. The kind of parody in which one writer mimics another, a little genre also known as "specific parody" or "literary parody," has been created by the parodic technique, but that technique has also been put to work to invent a cornucopia of other genres and nonliterary varieties of art.

My approach to parody presents the technique's three essential variations, and when you understand them, you will be in virtual possession of a recipe for generating these beauties. In fact, although the results may be messy, it's even possible to turn your life into a parody using the three basic maneuvers described below.

Here's my temporary definition (to be followed by a couple of add-ons at the end of this chapter):

> *Parody is a technique, probably hardwired in all of us, that tweaks, rechannels, transforms, or invents artistic conventions by* banging, binding, *or blending material into paired, unlikely contrasts. The result is art that is wildly dualistic. Because of the upheavals it creates, the parodic technique is the principal source of technical innovation and change in all the arts, the fountainhead of new genres and modes as well as the core of many masterpieces. Parody is the art that plays with art.*

For our purposes, a convention can be defined as any recurring element in art (or in communication per se) that, apart from its other features, meanings, and uses, can be isolated and treated as a mechanical unit of construction. If it can be isolated, the unit can also be parodized, that is, banged, bound, or blended into terms of contrast.

Along with being the principal breeder of novelty and change in the arts, parody is also the chief rehabilitator of what is old and worn out. It is also, if such is possible, a benevolent executioner: the technique that lays truly burned-out material to well-deserved rest also finds new ways to resurrect and rechannel such stuff—much like Hamburger Helper.

In the course of their aesthetic travels, parodists have created the modern novel, along with a very large number of artistic masterpieces. According to one authority or another (including me...what the hell?), parodists are responsible, fully or in part, for the development in the last few hundred years of such genres as nonsense, futurism, cubism, expressionism, Dadaism, surrealism, absurdist art, pop art, op art, conceptual art, and performance art, among others. In fact, most of the "isms" associated with modernism, a period of extreme aesthetic experimentation, whose heyday extends from roughly 1900 to 1970, owe their creation, all or in part, to parody. Modernism, by the way, isn't dead, even though it no longer dominates the cultural mainstream. When last seen, modernism was hiding out in Fort Deposit, Alabama.

To begin again: the three major variations or iterations of parody that appear, alone or in combination, *bang*, *bind*, and *blend* contrasting pairings. These iterations may function in a standalone fashion as seemingly distinct methods of parodic creation, but the variations also function as the components of a spectrum or continuum. The technique, as it marries paired contrasts, can mutate from crude to seamless iterations, and because the variations are part of a continuum, they may seem to melt into one another. Although parodic variations in their simplest manifestations are accessible to children, the applications quickly become convoluted and maze-like—an artistic hall of mirrors that may be as firmly resistant to sorting out as the tax code.

From a very young age, children seem to be active parodists. I believe, but certainly cannot prove, that the technique is hardwired in all of us, and by the time children reach nursery school or kindergarten, many are reasonably proficient playground parodists. Left to their own devices on a playground, some kids will typically utilize the *blending* variation to mimic others, most particularly, adult authority figures. Other children can frequently be found engaging in mock warfare, mock housekeeping, and the like *binding* elements that are purely kiddie concerns with elements from the adult world. And some will often find ways to *bang* their way to comic violence, injecting dirty words into their disquisitions or creating and then destroying sand castles or other playground edifices. If, by the way, you haven't done this sort of thing in a while, you are surely missing out on lots of fun and the opportunity to be committed to a psychiatric ward.

The skeletal, child-accessible basics of the parodic technique can be rendered with the simplest of diagrams:

PARODY

The Major Variations

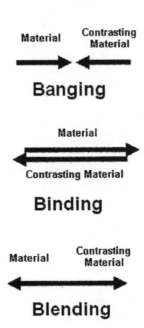

Material   Contrasting Material

→ ←

Banging

Material

⟷

Contrasting Material

Binding

Material   Contrasting Material

←→

Blending

The famous depiction by Honoré Daumier and Charles Philipon of France's King Louis Philippe evolving into a pear offers another way of envisioning the parodic technique at work:

This engraving actually parodizes the conventions of caricature, which is a parodic art in its own right—the initial portrayal of the king creates a sort of subliminal double image, an implicit contrast with more realistic potential images of Louis. Even if you are unfamiliar with this minor royal, your mind's eye will instantly realize that a *real* representation has been comically distorted. From that point forward and in the next three caricatures, the design increasingly stretches the conventions of this form until a pear emerges, which, if it appeared alone, would probably not be recognizable as King Louis.

In addition to demonstrating parodic metamorphosis, the components of the cartoon, with a bit of rearranging, can be mobilized to illustrate the three principal iterations of parody:

Banging = Violent Contrasts

Binding = Implausible Contrasts

Blending = Melded Contrasts

Some conventions lend themselves to parodization because they seem odd, quirky, extreme, or out-of-date, while others do not stand out particularly—apart from the fact that they can be paired readily with contrasting conventions and so banged, bound, or blended into parodic existence. I doubt that many of his contemporaries perceived that Louis Philippe had quirky features that resembled a pear until parody forged such a connection.

A contemporary engraving of the king supports this point, even though the graphic work, no doubt, is flattering:

And the moral, of course, is that we shouldn't rush to judgment based on pearances.

Parodists dine on an endless feast of material that lends itself to banging, binding, and blending. Even a brief survey will suggest the overarching reach of this methodology. I'll begin a micro-survey below with the simplest uses of the technical variations—in stand-up comedy—and proceed to more complicated examples. Most parodies employ all three variations simultaneously, but, for the purposes of this blindingly quick travelogue and in my dissections in succeeding chapters, I will focus on one variation at a time. The three majors each have two principal subiterations—a total of six. These subiterations, I also suspect, have their own offspring consisting of additional iterations, but with an exception or two, I haven't explored these depths here or elsewhere. My only excuse is that I am old and easily confused.

Bangs. Like those who enjoy blowing up then popping balloons, parodists utilize this variation to create and then to undermine a set of expectations by slapping them with radical alternatives. The bang is the operative force in standard-issue jokes—those with appropriately named punch lines. An example from Rodney Dangerfield: "When I was born, the doctor came out to the waiting room and said to my father, 'I'm very sorry. We did everything we could, but he pulled through.'"

This variation, the banging of conventional expectations, is the underlying methodology in slapstick, burlesque, and other kinds of physical comedies, such as those of the Keystone Cops and other early Hollywood comic legends right up through the Three Stooges. The banging methodology structures the verbal and physical comedy of the Marx Brothers, of Monty Python, and of all practitioners of the form known as nonsense. It is the force that vivifies the absurdity in the Theatre of the Absurd; it is the metaphysical pie that continually smacks the audience in surreal or Dadaesque works, in the "happenings" of the 1960s and 1970s, and in the "performance art" of today.

The two principal subvariations of parodic bangs are *disruptive bangs* and *conjoining bangs*. The former are what I've just been discussing, and they consist of stray explosions in works of literature and other arts. Conjoining bangs, when they are utilized, emerge in such profusion and/or with such similarity that they seem to take over the structure of a work and to endow it with something equivalent to a syncopated rhythm (as in Voltaire's *Candide*, in Joseph Heller's *Catch-22*, or in a meeting with an insurance salesman). Conjoining bangs are not tackled in this volume, so, other than pointing out their existence, I'll say no more about them—unless you find and waterboard me.

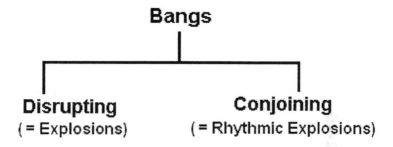

Bangs

Disrupting
(= Explosions)

Conjoining
(= Rhythmic Explosions)

Binds. Stand-up comics employ this variation when they address audience members directly, stepping reflexively outside the frame of the performance into the *real* world, as it were. "Reflexivity" refers to works that are aware of their own artiness and that, for instance, address the audience directly, such as in theatrical versions of *Peter Pan*, in Tony Richardson's film *Tom Jones*, in several of Woody Allen's films—and in the school pageant when Marjean wet her pants.

The major subiterations of parodic binds are *bunched binding*, in which the targeted terms of contrast are simply thrown together helter-skelter (as in comic epics) so that the process resembles stuffing a sausage skin, and *banded binding*, in which the terms of contrast are presented as alternatives in layers or nests, such as stories-within-stories and other varieties of narrative embedding.

Bunch-bound parodies, like the wildly off-key but nonjarring mating of conventional antitheses in a typical mock epic, may simply scatter inappropriate or unlikely pairings in no particular order and with no evident plan. Bunched binds, unlike parodic bangs, do not produce explosive contrasts, and after generating initial surprise, these crazed pairings can begin to seem oddly normal—as in the kind of writing known as "magic realism."

Banded binding is more orderly than its bunched counterparts. If an embedded work is parodic, there is an ambiguous relationship between levels of narration, between stories and frames, and between other nesting levels of *reality* embedded like Chinese boxes or Russian nested dolls. This variation of the parodic technique, however, like conjunctive bangs, is also beyond the scope of this book. To find out more, you'll have to read my other volume or await the Rapture.

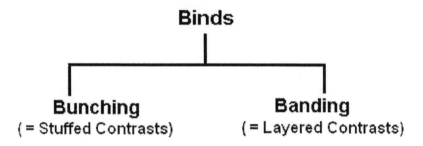

Blends. Finally, there are two major subiterations of parodic blending, the most subtle, complicated, and misunderstood components in the parodist's arsenal:

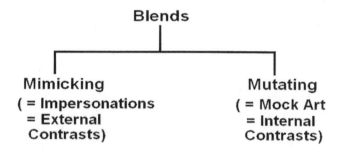

Mimicking blends impersonate someone or something that is specific, identifiable, and definite, such as a public figure, a best-selling novel, or a popular film. When a comic performs a dead-on impression of a notable politician or other celebrity, the parodic blending variation has made an appearance. The effect is smooth and seamless. And it is a nearly impossible task to sort out the plural creation that emanates from some foggy border between the imitator and the imitatee. Almost everyone has a built-in ability to unleash this kind of mimicry now and then. It is a universal tendency. But for all its overwhelming frequency, first-rate mimicry is very, very difficult to do well, a fact that seems to be lost on many authorities who attempt to analyze parody.

More sophisticated versions of such blending are the comic send-ups in specific or literary parody, the kind of writing that most readers think of as "parody." In great literary parodies, a Max Beerbohm, a Wolcott Gibbs, or a Peter DeVries comically reproduces Kipling, or Hemingway, or Faulkner for purposes that range from ridicule to reverence. The best examples of such mimicry generate a ghostly, illusionistic dualism, and in the hands of the gifted, such as Beerbohm, Frederick Crews, and various *New Yorker* writers, the net effect is like a brilliant jazz riff on a well-known piece of music.

Specific parody can (and does) generate legal disputes about plagiarism and copyright violations, so there is at least some basis, however wrongheaded, for raising questions about the originality of parody. Fortunately for parodists, the courts, citing the Fair Use Doctrine, have usually come down on their side.

But mimicry is only one of the six major iterative applications of parody. None of the other five conform to or fit the blanket definition that all forms of parody amount to copycat imitation or parasitism—nor, for that matter, do any of the other traditional little parodic genres, such as mock epic or burlesque.

Another way of approaching the absurd, widespread belief that *all* parody is secondhand borrowing is to consider the matter from a legal standpoint. If a parodic work lacks specifically identifiable mimicry or dense specific allusion, it simply would not be considered actionable. But, even so, if some rich lunatic believes that he owns the rights to mock epics, say, and insists on protecting his stake, the case would be summarily dismissed, if not laughed out of court in the same way that a claim to ownership of the moon or stars would be expelled.

As a variation of blending, mimicry has also been utilized to create such additional genres as pastiche and Literary Imitation, which include works that can be longer and more serious than specific parodies and that may be considered grown-up versions of specific parody. Further, various free translations and adaptations also qualify as mimicry—if dualistic, illusionistic contrasts are part of their mix. Mimicry, as I've indicated, is severely undervalued and misunderstood, but it also must be admitted that relatively few classics or towering works of art fall within its ranks.

The real action in parody springs from *blended parodic mutations*, and parodists employing this variation have produced shelves full of innovative masterpieces. As the most important variation of this transforming *über*-technique, parodic mutations can inform limitless kinds of works with varying degrees of complexity and importance.

Mimicking blends generate contrasts with external models, but the contrasts in mutated blends are, in every meaningful sense, internally generated. In mutations, the parodist plays with the innards of his or her own work, somewhat in the manner of a conscientious attorney who utterly transforms the conventions of home life by billing his or her family for "quality time."

Unfortunately, there has been no litcrit apparatus or expert commentary to deal with parodic mutations. The category simply doesn't exist as far as aesthetic theory is concerned. To remedy this unfortunate situation, I have tried in my scholarly book to develop some descriptive language and terminology to encompass parodic mutations. Again, these works transform whatever they touch into dualities—their plots, their styles, their manner of narration, their genres.

Above all, it should be absolutely understood that mutated blends deserve to be recognized as original compositions in the same way that any work of art is, until contrary evidence is mustered. To think otherwise is akin to believing in such absurdities as bodily humours, a flat earth, or a merry Christmas.

In the case of mutated blends, parodists depart from "imitation," in the sense of any specific indebtedness, and create highly colored, highly ambiguous, or highly disguised art of various sorts, including hoaxes, such as Swift's famous mock pamphlet, "A Modest Proposal." Parodic hoaxes and faux "histories," such as *Gulliver's Travels*, *Moll Flanders*, and *Robinson Crusoe*, were instrumental stepping-stones in the formation of formal realism in modern fiction, and all of these works feature parodic mutation as the dominant piece of technical architecture.

Since the eighteenth century, parody has underwritten a host of storytellers, novelists particularly, who specialize in seamless but highly ambiguous mock fictions containing equally ambiguous narration, all of which fosters parodically multiple interpretations. Works of fiction, especially experimental examples associated with modernism and postmodernism (modernism's playful successor), tend to be permeated with variations of the parodic technique—with blended mutation generally leading the way.

A relatively simple variety of fiction that blended mutation produces is what I call "general parody spoofs." Most parodies in *The New Yorker* these days, those that appear in the "Shouts and Murmurs" department, are general parody spoofs in the form of mock essays, mock short stories, epistles, newsletters, pamphlets, and broadsides. Until now, these have been invariably mistaken for specific parodies, but typically they contain only a whiff or two of mimicry and so deserve to be treated as original works by any reasonable standard.

These, then, are just some of the many fruits of blended parodic mutations:

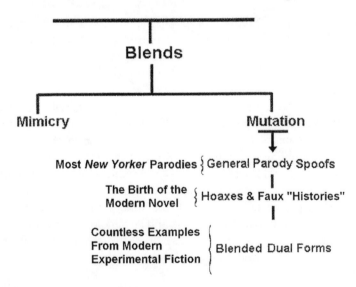

Experimental writing that I call "blended dual forms" will not be examined in the chapters ahead—with the exception of the final chapter, which dives into the making of modernist poetry. The chapters on blending will focus on specific parody and general parody spoofs. That material should be more than enough for beginners to explore—and the effort will be a lot more fun than studying up on the Hundred Years' War or the Ninety-Minute Spat.

A final but most important point: the parodic technique, by way of its dualistic contrasts and multiple mazes, creates "multistable art," meaning art that invites multiple interpretations and wholly reversible frames of reference—as in this famous example that can be perceived alternatively as a rabbit and a duck:

Thus far, I think, the fact that parody creates multistable art remains wholly unrecognized and unexplored by most authorities. For the record, I maintain that *all* multistable art is parodic, that such art is, in fact, the hallmark of parody.

Such reversible dualism, in turn, may also help explain why parody, like Rodney Dangerfield, has gotten no respect: in recorded history, the parodic technique has been downright subversive. Parody not only paints moustaches on the *Mona Lisa*, but also lurks as a major alternative to 2,500 years of orderly, stable Western logic and logical ways of analysis.

However, the climate of opinion vis-à-vis parody may already have begun to change. Reflexive art, for instance, has garnered much respectful theoretical attention in recent years. Self-aware art, which I prefer to call "reflexive art," is also always parodic, and I suggest further that reflexive art, which dances back and forth between the boundaries separating art from life, is a special case of multistable art, which means it offers extraordinary illusionistic potential in its art-vs.-life dualism.

All in all, in the realm of literature (and in the other arts, for that matter), we have been living in an age of parody. Even so, the force and breadth of parody is not recognized by many readers or explained very effectively by literary scholars and theorists—some of whom, however, do frequently agree at least that parody is the central ingredient in this modernist/ postmodernist period. So, now it's up to you to write parody that will astonish the world and provide assurance that this category is given its proper due alongside cures for halitosis and jock itch.

Thus ends my general explanation of parody and, temporarily, my rants. And here, is a composite representation of the parodic technique:

THE PARODIC TECHNIQUE

Parody

Bangs		Binds		Blends	
Disrupting (= Explosions)	Conjoining (= Rhythmic Explosions)	Bunching (= Stuffed Contrasts)	Banding (= Layered Contrasts)	Mimicking (= Impersonations = External Contrasts)	Mutating (= Mock Art = Internal Contrasts)

Artistic Conventions

Conventional Contrasts & Multistability & Reflexivity

> Traditional Parodic Genres
> Non Traditional Parodic Genres
> Free Form Parody In All the Arts

And here again is my definition of parody—with the extra ingredients added:

Parody is a technique, probably hardwired in all of us, that tweaks, rechannels, transforms, or invents artistic conventions by banging, binding, *or* blending *material into paired, unlikely contrasts. The result is art that is wildly dualistic, multistable, and frequently reflexive. Because of the upheavals it creates, the parodic technique is the principal source of technical innovation and change in all the arts, the fountainhead of new genres and modes as well as the core of many masterpieces. Parody is the art that plays with art.*

2.

Parody Tartare

As I've said, I'm convinced that most of us are born parodists. For those who think they have lost the knack, this parody instruction manual might help restore the kind of childhood parodic invention that was once a virtually automatic part of your verbal and histrionic arsenal. I believe that parodic nerve cells still survive in the majority of otherwise no-nonsense adults, even if the synapses have stopped emitting signals and the cells have shriveled from long disuse.

I've indicated that the recipe for parody requires you, as a budding parodist, to create contrasting pairings—pairings of single words, of concepts, of ways of communicating, the more the better. There can almost never be too many such pairings. Further, these pairings should be mismatched. Signs of harmony, normally desirable in works of art, are banned from most parodies. Parodic pairings should be inappropriate, disparate, out-of-kilter, antithetical, illogical, and/or absurd.

The term *parody*, by the way, stems from the ancient Greek noun, παρωδια (*parodia* is the Latin translation), meaning "a beside-or-against song." Here, in addition to music, "song" denotes a poem, and beside-or-against songs referred originally to ancient comic and mock epics. The original derivation accurately describes what the parodic technique accomplishes: in parody, two or more terms of contrast are always in unlikely play beside or against one another.

I hope my commentary thus far has not made parody sound forbiddingly complicated and difficult. The complexity is there all right, but it emerges all by itself from the simple injection of the accessible applications of an easy-to-apply technique. As a parodist, you don't need to strategize about how to generate dazzling and confounding illusions in your work. That fancy stuff will emerge as a natural by-product of your efforts—like fruit growing, ripening, and falling off a tree or like the buildup and completion of a great bowel movement.

Keep in mind how simple it is to create parody. The parodist gathers material (a.k.a. conventions) that can be made to clash, that can be lashed together, however odd the pairing, or that can be merged into or alongside contrasting material with only a ripple or two to suggest that something is askew.

This description, of course, does not cover gritty specifics, the hand-to-hand combat of actually putting a parody together. So it's time now for a full-scale example followed by a dissection of how it has been constructed. My chosen example, "Flea Markets and Flea Enterprise," is about 1,300 words long. Most of the other examples I've included in this book also fall within the range of 1,000 to 1,500 words. That's the length of most short parodies that have made their way into print in these times, the general parody spoofs that I plan to focus on.

So here is Parodic Example I:

FLEA MARKETS AND FLEA ENTERPRISE

Depression ahead??????—NAAAHH!!!!!!! Sales Will Be Swell *after Two Thousand and Twelve!!!!!!!!!!!!!!!!!!!!!!!!!!!!!!!*

So let's all pitch in and fight Industrial Decay just like our "Pals Across the Waters," the "Limeys," did, by selling bits and pieces of ourselves, our pasts and our futures. But we don't have to be Nit-Brits about that process, because we've got American sales and marketing knowhow. Here's how The Magic will keep coming back.

Our friends in "Yankee Land" tell us that next season the antique mobile home market will really start rolling. Insiders expect this dynamite combination to lead the way—look for lots of Peterbilt "Big Rigs" to pull an array of mobilized New England saltbox houses. The saltbox, by the way, has been a popular roadhouse since old "Cal" Coolidge, a dead but sexy ex-Prexy, ran out of gas in one. You'll want to lay in lots of Vermont Blue Saltboxes along with your Rhode Island Reds.

And what about stuffed dogs! We look for these cute little critters to worm their way back into your hearts and minds (oh, yes, they're housebroken). Antique dog fanciers will snub your old-timey Victorian models with the glass presentation cases and all that crushed velvet. Nowadays a spiffy-looking model rates a simulated "Green Eco-System" with cranberry sauce and all the trimmings. Note: a few of your customers may want to hold onto their poochies, but you should be able to convince the rest that "antiquing" is the best way to get some extra mileage from that beat-up piece of canine equipment or from that "sleeper" down at the doggie pound.

It looks like an all-around good year for animals. At the top of most shopping lists are live saber-tooth tigers—*tres* popular and *tres* expensive because they're very, very extinct. To get your own live beasties in your own live flea market booth, simply budget a little time for attaching sabers to your tiger kittens or tigers onto your saber seedlings.

Letters, we get letters. Mr. Hester Morton of Walloon Lake, Michigan, writes, "I am simply twenty three years old as of the current year in process, but I am willing to budget a little time to become a flea marketeer right away if somebody will let me trade up for some interesting old-timey baseball cards. I am looking for a raspberry-flavored Wally Moon, a midnight blue Mel Parnell, and a 'Bullet Bob' Turley with an oak leaf cluster." Good luck, Hester. Don't take any wooden Cleveland Indians.

Surprised? Sure we were, but we've had to admit that there still seems to be a hard market for the Treasure of the Pharaohs. It's now illegal to pass through Utah without ponying up some tax bullion for your basalt sacred cats, and according to the latest SAMI reports, three hundred and eleven carloads of golden ankhs were shipped from the Boise-Cascade area last month (the bombshell marketing theme: Ankhs for the Memory!).

Whoops, we're the people who predicted two years ago that the gears of this industry would be stripped because the supply was running out. Well, our faces are red, but we're out there on a limb again, flashing a green light. We're bullish now because us Insiders got tipped off at the Pharaoh Godmother Convention in Minneapolis. Psst...by next November casks of Egyptian Treasure will begin bubbling up through a hole in Iowa.

Back to basics: sell anything relating to Argentina. Mr. Sizemore Balzer of Elk Grove Village, Illinois, has a nephew visiting those foreigners right this very minute, and he already knows, in the biblical sense, large chunks of the Pampas. And we hear he's about to lock down rights to an "Evita" Peron Tofu franchise that features boiled, never oleaginous, never fried, Antique Bean Curd. This is an outfit with a commitment to health trumpeted by the franchise's brand-new theme song, "Don't Fry for Me, Argentina."

You might also want to market anything related to Panama, even though thousands of anti-biz Commies might try to stand in your way. Try removing the Commies with ant and roach paste, and if you succeed, well, we wish you a Merry Isthmus.

Some more words to the wise: do your best to market the latest brand-*new* antiques, and don't get trapped by out of date items: that traditional stuff is frequently old and very dirty.

And sometimes dangerous. The late Mrs. LaVerne Goeth of Upsala LA tried to "jazz up" her wedding by providing all the standard traditional trappings: an *old* derelict with *new* dentures had been *borrowed* and painted *blue* for the occasion by Earl ("I will still paint any derelict blue for $29.95") Slab. Well, to make it short and sweet, the derelict drop-kicked his pretty little sponsor over the carport.

But there's a silver lining to the casket, so to speak. The last photos of the Dear-Departed are now collector's items. You can get yours from Earl Slab's Body Shop. The pics are embedded in Lucite, and they're framed along with a snappy, moralistical caption: "Bride Goeth Before a Fall."

And speaking of death, another good marketing item is pomes that you yourself have written and planted in dirt and mulch (for seasoning and in case an editor demands some cuttings).

Right now, we're "grooving" on the work of Ms. Jo Bobbi McClure. She writes, "Antiques and Junque should be expensive, so I have written a pome about my late husband. When living, he was always high, now he's stiff." Her offering:

Commode for Joe Bob

The cold world once menaced
a plumber's apprentice—
Joe Bob McClure is dead.
He went for a snake
and made a mistake
and brought back a rattler instead.
But flush out your eyes—
somewhere in the skies,
there are angels
at work on God's sewers.
And all white and pure
is Joe Bob McClure.
He's the Great Plumber's Helper
for sure.

Fortissimo, Ms. McClure. Send us a few more pomes like "Commode for Joe Bob," and we'll turn into your biggest roto-rooters.

Well, Guys and Gals, that's about all the fresh news we have on tap, and, even tho the stale news is getting more valuable by the minute, we'll begin winding down with a few gobs of personal advice to Our Faithful Readers:

- ☻ Memo to J. H: Don't buy no more antique rocks grown in the Ural Mountains. That market has peaked.

- ☻ A thought for C. K: Why do we recommend antiques as your flea market merchandise of choice? Because antiques are a subsidiary of The Past, one of the few "heavy" industries with a guaranteed annual rate of growth.

- ☻ Flash to R. N: Collect anything Greek. There's a goldmine in the Attic.

- ☻ Confidential to Dr. R. K: Ok, go ahead and scrape out antique infected tonsils for your collection, but remember that some squealing "Deep Throat" is going to accuse you of strep-mining.

☻ A word of encouragement for N. C: Sure, it takes a long time to build up a big antiques inventory, but the act of *not* collecting antiques takes a lot longer.

A Parting Shot:
Here's the top secret that all of you have been asking about. How do we keep on trucking with such high energy from show to show, newsletter to newsletter, drive-by shooting to drive-by shooting? What is it, after all, that we are driven to collect?

We've unwrapped this secret in a pome that we ourselves have written and wrapped in seedlings and planted in dirt and mulch so that fertility will be restored to the land:

> We never buzz off on safari
> after hunks of old Imari
> when we can lope down to a village
> snarfing mounds of human spillage,
> nostalgic chunks of candy bars—
> your antique Peanut Butter Cup,
> your Mars.
> Man's hopes and dreams
> should not be tested
> until the Past has been digested.

And that really is it for now, or, as they say in the antique Italian trucking business, "That's-a-haul-folks."

* * *

You may have noticed that this little essay is full of puns—loaded with them. Puns are nuclear units of parody. Puns, as dictionaries explain rather ponderously, are forged by a play on words, sometimes on different senses of the same word and sometimes on the similar sense or sound of different words. In punnic arrangements, the material is forcibly banged, bound, and blended, and the crazed pairings that result are the real point of the exercise.

So, unlike metaphors (with which they can be confused) puns do not aim for shared likenesses or identities in their pairings. Parodies, including puns, emphasize the often outrageously divergent dualities of their terms of contrast, their lack of oneness. Metaphors tend to be stable, puns multistable. The extraordinary contrasts of the latter can be as radically dualistic as language itself will permit.

Consider the punning examples that appear in the graceful poem you have just read:

Commode for Joe Bob
The cold world once menaced
a plumber's apprentice:
Joe Bob McClure is dead.
He went for a *snake*
and made a mistake:
he brought back a rattler instead.
But *flush out your eyes*.
somewhere in the skies
there are Angels at work on God's sewers,
and all white and pure is Joe Bob McClure.
He's *the Great Plumber's Helper*, for sure.

Obviously, there are several compressed punnic pairings here. "Commode" in the title suggests both "ode" and "toilet." "Snake" incorporates both a plumber's snake, a tool that will wind through meandering pipes and unclog them, and an actual reptile. "Flush out your eyes" refers both to washing away tears or strain and, in this context, to flushing a toilet. And, finally, "the Great Plumber's Helper" encompasses, on one hand, the Almighty and Joe Bob's new titular role, and, on the other, a stick with a rubber bulb that can be compressed and then expanded to dislodge excremental toilet blockades.

Puns, as nuclear units of parody, frequently use all three chief variations of the parodic technique simultaneously. And the three variations can appear, not just concisely, but with extreme compression. I recently spotted a bumper sticker that illustrates what I mean. It reads, "Visualize Whirled Peas." The parody seamlessly mimics and evokes another bumper sticker, one that seems to appear everywhere. That familiar bumper sticker recommends the New Age magic that will presumably transpire if only people-kind become willing to "Visualize World Peace."

In the parodic bumper sticker, two wholly unrelated admonitions have been smoothly melded together, the seamlessness exemplifying the blending iteration. At the same time, two ridiculously different subjects—world peace and whirled peas—have been yoked together, which is simultaneously a case of binding. Third, the incongruity of this parodic package, the mild shock that hits most people when they suddenly *get* the pun, is an instance of parodic banging. Such witty inclusiveness and compression qualifies puns like this one to be deemed parodic royalty.

My claim that all three variations of the technique are present in the Whirled Peas pun can be disputed by the counter-claim that I have merely applied three different bits of nomenclature to what is just a single technique, a play on words that sound alike but that have wholly different meanings. I admit that, in the Whirled Peas pun, the parodic variations have all seemed to coalesce, and their individual contributions must be extrapolated, but this is simply a clear indication that (a) the parodic technique incorporates a spectrum, and as a result, (b) its components are potentially evanescent, spectral, and illusory, and as a further result, (c) each component can seem to fold into the others and, if the parodist so desires, unfold back out again.

I believe that this tripartite, spectral quality of parody is overlooked by most readers and viewers of parody, who focus instead on the parodic variation that seems to be most important in a given work. In fact, each major variation of the parodic technique—banging, binding, and blending—can function in individual works as standalone architecture that dominates all facets of the work, a condition that is demonstrable in countless examples. It simply doesn't occur to most people that a single technique embodies multiple variations and that these can be shuffled and made to appear, to disappear, or to merge like props in a magic show.

That's enough for the moment about puns, but now you know my dirty little secret: despite the near-universal groaning they provoke, puns are parodic royalty, and I love them.

In assessing the little parody above, you should begin by deciding what genre or genres (in addition to the familiar little forms known as "parody") you've encountered. Frequently, as in this example, a parody consists of several generic overlays. Freedom to mix and mingle should make your job easier. If you hit a dead end with one type of writing, you can jump to another.

"Flea Markets" combines nonfiction, a faux newsletter, with the sort of anarchic comedy known as burlesque. But its most important generic overlay is nonsense, a purely parodic invention, as I have noted, and this is a genre that I strongly recommend for parodic novices. The chief demand laid on a nonsense work is that it not make much sense (but just enough to keep the game going and the reader interested). In complying with this loose mandate, the nonsense work also need not display much evidence of unity or coherence beyond a decipherable starting point and a termination—usually quite abrupt—that shuts the enterprise down, ideally, with a parodic flourish, such as an utterly pointless pun. Even a beginner should have no trouble compiling this semi-aimless, semi-meaningless mixture.

As a rule, the chief feature of much nonsense is dense parodic banging, that most thoroughly accessible of the parodic variations:

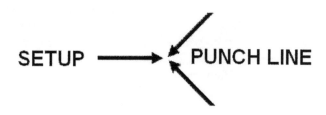

Parodic Banging 101

Basic parodic bangs (disruptive bangs) need be no more sophisticated than a verbal explosion (or two or thirty-three) in a given work. In a step up from there, bangs consist of one-liners, a methodology that is probably as ancient as spoken language itself. With such bangs, an intelligible, reasonable premise of some sort is established (the setup) and, by one means or another, the setup is incongruously violated, routed, or exploded by countering it violently with the punch line (an aptly-named term if there ever was one).

The range of punch lines varies wildly. Punch lines can emerge from displays of wit, here meaning imaginative or intellectual ingenuity (including punning and wordplay), and they can consist of sledge-hammer blows of crudity, profanity, scatology, and the like. Whatever their origin, punch lines can be expected to dismantle or disorient—in startling ways— the provisions of the setups that precede them.

The "Flea Market" parody is inundated with one-liners, including those that offer the full package, formal setups followed by formal punch lines:

[**Setup**] Why do we recommend antiques as your flea market merchandise of choice?
[**Punch line**] Because antiques are a subsidiary of The Past, one of the few "heavy" industries with a guaranteed annual rate of growth.

[**Setup**] Sure, it takes a long time to build a big antiques inventory, [**Punch line**] but the act of *not* collecting antiques takes a lot longer.

Even more prevalent in the little parody are one-liners in which the setup is merely implicit or one-liners that ramble a bit until the punch line explodes out of nowhere in a more or less leisurely fashion. For example, this advice occurs at the tail end of a passage that advocates the marketing of antique mobile homes, including "mobilized New England saltbox houses":

You'll want to lay in lots of Vermont Blue Saltboxes along with your Rhode Island Reds.

Rhode Island Reds are a breed of chicken.

As parodic bangs, one-liners are generally expected to be funny or witty. But nonsense is a genre in which banging non sequiturs and other jolts of illogic generally suffice to camouflage an overall lack of professional comic material. In other words, nonsense is a forgiving genre, one in which a novice can get along without being terribly humorous.

A passage such as the following from "Flea Markets," for example, is pretty lame. Its pertinence here stems from the absurdity and impossibility of the material and not from the weak, out-of-the-blue pun:

> You might also want to market anything related to Panama, even though thousands of anti-biz Commies might try to stand in your way. Try removing the Commies with ant and roach paste, and, if you succeed, well, we wish you a Merry Isthmus.

Similarly, another passage in the parody contains the implicit setup that brides on their wedding day are supposed to wear something old, something new, something borrowed, and something blue. For "something blue," the passage alludes, as an implicit setup, to a long-running advertisement by the Earl Scheib chain of automobile painting franchises:

> The late Mrs. LaVerne Goeth of Upsala LA tried to "jazz up" her wedding by providing all the standard traditional trappings: An old derelict with new dentures had been borrowed and painted blue for the occasion by Earl ("I will still paint any derelict blue for $29.95") Slab.

Again, the passage hardly reflects world-class wit, and it's certainly not laugh-out-loud funny, but this sort of thing can enable a novice to get all the way through a passable first parody or two or three.

"Flea Markets and Flea Enterprise" utilizes another ingredient that is novice-friendly. It has a narrative style that is slangy, sloppy, palsy-walsy, intrusive, overly familiar, and clearly insincere. Above all, the narration is reflexive, which, again, is art that is self-aware and that is, in this case, art that is both phony and seemingly very conscious of its own slightly repulsive phoniness. If asked to give this style a name (and at the risk of seeming pretentious), I would probably call it "reflexive Babbittry," after the title character in Sinclair Lewis's novel, *Babbitt*, a glad-handing, mega-tacky, Midwestern realtor.

Reflexive art is a good choice for novices because it is easy to create (there are lots of ways to let readers know that they are in on the game as you play with the narrative) and because reflexivity offers an instant kind of sophisticated duality whenever it appears in a work. As I've explained, reflexive art is always parodic. As a result of such parodic play, reflexivity actively demonstrates that it is double-edged, that it is dancing between the realms of art and nonart. And although reflexivity as a tactic does not appeal to all members of art's audience, the tactic is, nonetheless, an automatic source of art-vs.-life conundrums and a complicating factor that smacks of high-level artistic gamesmanship.

Reflexive art also can be highly self-protective, a means of sheltering a novice from his or her beginner's mistakes. In other words, a few patches of genuinely bad writing can be masked by *intentionally* bad writing, an overall approach that winks at the presumably literate reader and shares with the reader an in-joke about how amusing terrible prose can be. Thus the narration in "Flea Markets" opts for aggressively *bad* writing replete with clichés, corny slang, and stupid spelling and punctuation tricks. Examples:

- "Cal" Coolidge, a dead but sexy ex-Prexy
- a simulated "Green Eco-System" with cranberry sauce and all the trimmings
- anti-biz Commies
- Well, to make it short and sweet
- Right now, we're "grooving" on the work of Ms. Jo Bobbi McClure
- we'll turn into your biggest roto-rooters
- a few gobs of personal advice to Our Faithful Readers

Another confession: I enjoy creating this kind of awful prose and find it a welcome, if occasional, relief from seriousness. There's a nursery in my hometown that, in its advertising proclaims, as a primary benefit, that its customers get "to play in the dirt again." *Bad* parodic stylistics amount to the same kind of mud mucking for me and, no doubt, shields some of my weaknesses.

For all its relative accessibility, "Flea Market" has reasonably complicated architecture if it is taken apart. The content depends heavily on parodic banging:

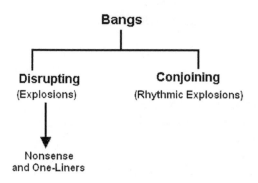

Parodic Banging
in "Flea Markets"

The parody's structure consists of a skein of contrasts between its absurd description of antiques and marketing and, implicitly, real antiques and real marketing:

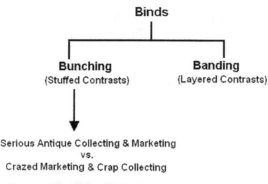

**Parodic Binding
in "Flea Markets"**

Finally, the style and narration evolve from a general parody spoof of a normal newsletter imparted in a manner I've described as "reflexive Babbitry":

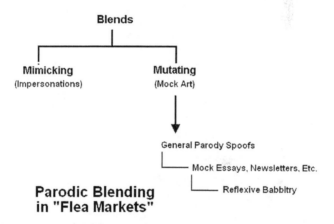

**Parodic Blending
in "Flea Markets"**

The technical array in "Flea Markets and Flea Enterprise" is typical of parody. As a rule of thumb, the banging technique is particularly useful in generating parodic content; binding is often enlisted to fashion structural architecture; and blending is often mobilized as a principal resource in formulating style and narration. That said, I must immediately add that *all* the technical iterations of parody can appear anywhere in a work, adding extra dimensions wherever they pop up.

Summary. A parody such as "Flea Markets and Flea Enterprise" is a bit like a five-finger exercise, and you, the beginning parodist, should not hesitate to attempt something similar. You need to create a multitude of contrasts, and I recommend that you bundle them into all three of the major iterations of the parodic technique. In doing so, I also recommend further that you choose a writer-friendly genre such as nonsense and a writer-protecting style such as one featuring loosey-goosey reflexivity.

3.

Listing Toward Parody

I'm sure that there are umpteen ways to begin gun slinging with the parodic technique, but arming yourself with two lists is a reliable method of getting underway. The first list I use is scattershot, a collection of paired contrasts more or less relating to the projected parodic subject. My second list is more thorough, a semi-schematic compilation based in part on the results produced from my first collection.

The initial list doesn't have to be anything other than snippets of private shorthand arranged into parodic pairings. In its barest form, the list can be likened to a compass that will do little more than tell you to head north or southwest. The first list, then, is also the equivalent of finger painting or fooling around with modeling clay. The aim is to jot down whatever comes to mind—with no thoughts of permanence. The preliminary list should simply collect batches of contrasting material. If you're lucky, your listed parodic pairings will begin to stack up into a pattern and to suggest ever more helpful details about the parodic Land of Oz that you're stumbling toward:

PARODY	
TOPIC	**CONTRAST**
Blah, Blah, Blah	**Anti-Blah, Blah, Blah**

Here, for example, is a list I put together for an aborted attempt to bunch bind a reality TV show with far more serious subject matter:

PARODY	
TOPIC	CONTRAST
World War II Japanese Mayhem	*The Real Housewives of New York*
Pearl Harbor	Jill drapes surviving ships in black organza
The Baatan Death March	LuAnn angrily ships her etiquette book to the Emperor and Prime Minister Tojo
Kamikaze Attacks	Kelly accuses Alex of inventing the idea

I assume it's self-evident why this particular project went nowhere.

I'm sure that a listing approach or some variation on it has been employed by zillions of parodists since ancient times—if only in the form of mental notes. I discovered, for instance, when I took a couple of stand-up comedy courses from a professional comedian, Jeff Justice, that he, too, recommends making comedic lists of paired contrasts.

However, Justice has a specific recipe in mind for this exercise. On his Web site, he offers directions for writing comic top-ten lists of the sort that have long been a staple of David Letterman's nightly TV show (see http://jeffjustice.com./topten.htm).

Justice suggests picking a subject (implicitly, one with inherent comic potential) and making "a list of everything you can think of regarding this subject, especially nouns or phrases." Next he prescribes, again implicitly, uncovering an adjective that describes an incongruous facet of the chosen subject and then making a second list of "everything that you can think of that has to do with" the incongruity. Finally, you should "choose one item from each group and put [the two] together with a little exaggeration to form your idea."

This process, of course, leads to the creation of a group of parodic pairings, and the approach has applications that extend far beyond top-ten lists. This methodology—creating a list and a counter-list—for all its simplicity, is a superb way to generate not only garden-variety parodic bangs, but the formula also offers a jump-start for creating mock fiction, works of bunched binding, and other parodic iterations.

For example, the subject Justice chooses on his Web site is the Rolling Stones, and the overall parodic duality is that (a) rock bands are supposed to epitomize orgiastic youthfulness, but (b) the Stones are old and creaky. Justice puts list 1 and list 2 together to arrive at a collection of suggested parodic titles for a Rolling Stones tour, including "The Brown Sugar and Bran Tour."

I hope that you, as a budding parodist, will incorporate a list-creating strategy. Ideally, preliminary lists should be started before the first draft of your parody. The key to getting underway is to generate or to stumble on a strong initial premise derived from the list. The premise should be (1) incongruous and (2) fertile, meaning that it should readily suggest strings of additional parodic pairings. If the premise fails to meet both of these requirements, then the parody that emerges may be less than satisfactory, the results stillborn.

The premise can be wild or absolutely impossible. The premise behind the mini-list I created above, for instance, assumes that bickering, narcissistic *arrivistes*, the now mostly purged cast of *The Real Housewives of New York*, have been named jointly and anachronistically to some important World War II posts, such as President Franklin Roosevelt's press aides.

Another premise with list potential is this one: imagine that the fictional cannibal and serial killer Dr. Hannibal Lecter has opened a rare book store. Naturally, it would feature dismembered or mutilated first editions, and the works on hand would include such titles as *A Farewell to Arms, Naked Lunch, Red Harvest, Things Fall Apart, The Executioner's Song, The Naked and the Dead, Wise Blood, Slaughterhouse Five, The Big Sleep, As I Lay Dying, Appointment in Samarra*, and *Blood Meridian*.

Still another premise: Jack Bauer, the hyperviolent, world-saving hero of the now-defunct TV series *24* has retired and become a dentist. The possibilities that emerge are multiple. His instrumentation, for instance, might include an ice pick, a blowtorch, a miniature jackhammer, or a surface-to-air missile.

I apologize for seeming so bloody-minded with these examples. But they do make my point forcibly.

You can, of course, jot down your lists on anything handy: napkins, brown paper bags, significant others. But I think that more of a green eyeshade, anal retentive approach is a better idea.

After compiling a preliminary list, I recommend that the ideas behind its choicest fruits be transferred to a second list, one that functions more formally to guide you through the creation of your parody. For me, among the benefits of using a work sheet or blueprint is that it helps disarm my tendency to thrash around with procedural minutiae and to embrace other symptoms of writer's block rather than getting to work. I often run through several work sheets in the process of creating a parody.

On the other hand, I occasionally find, during the initial stages of parodic creation, that a preliminary list alone suits me best, and for a while I put off using my parody work sheet. Sometimes an obligation to fill out a more formal document ahead of my writing and/or to adhere to the program I've laid out in that document, however tentatively, can have an inhibiting effect, even a stifling one, on my ability to free associate and to range all over the landscape of my mind, such as it is, to wrestle loose a parody. *But* I always fill out the work sheet completely when I've completed a first draft. At that point, a completed work sheet can be a major aid during the process of revision, a way of keeping you on track.

I have printed a blank form of my parody work sheet below. If the format suits you, I suggest you make copies of it, and use them to jot down your own plans for parodic creation.

Parody Work Sheet
TITLE

VARIATIONS

Bangs: Yes No Major Minor	Binds: Yes No Major Minor	Blends: Yes No Major Minor

ITERATIVE DETAILS
STYLISTIC / NARRATIONAL CONTRASTS

FORMAL / STRUCTURAL CONTRASTS

OTHER CONTRASTS

COMMENTS

Again, I strongly recommend that you adapt a listing format (but, of course, you should change it or mold it to suit your preferences). However, I must warn you that, should you vary from the format I have suggested, you run the very real risk of eternal damnation.

4.

How to Write Parodies–Plan B

What if, despite my suggestions thus far, you don't feel able to carve out a parody of your own? If that's the case, then let's shift to Plan B. The best Plan B advice I can offer is to point you in the direction of an example-based old time religion that's now lost—it's the way that writing was once taught to our ancestors.

A trigonometric function (if such a thing actually exists) copied repeatedly will remain impenetrable and mystifying. But a parody, if it's transcribed, can produce highly practical results. The act of copying and recopying all or part of a parody can inject parody into your writerly bloodstream.

Of course there's a bit more involved than repetitive copying. Benjamin Franklin had minimal formal education (his parents jerked him out of school at age ten), but he claims in his *Autobiography* that he taught himself to become a professional writer by performing the sorts of drills that were once part of everyone's education. He devised imitative parodic and semi-parodic exercises using some of *The Spectator* essays by Joseph Addison and Richard Steele. And Ben never abandoned parody. As a mature writer, he produced many clever parodic hoaxes.

It helps, obviously, to have Franklin's genius; nonetheless, the writing of our non-genius ancestors tends to be far less embarrassing than most of our limp modern effusions. And for nearly two thousand years our forebears learned writing skills by copying, then parodically imitating exemplary texts on their way to flying off on their own.

There are an infinite number of places to find material worth parodizing. A readily available starting point, for instance, is the "Goings On About Town" section of *The New Yorker* magazine. It features old and new mini-versions of stylistically intricate film reviews by that magazine's past and present reviewers. The verbal cartwheels of these writers, transposed into parodic contexts of your own devising, will enable you to begin creating your own parodized gymnastics.

Another approach is (a) to see or read a quirky film, play, or text and (b) with the quirks fresh in your mind write your own parodic response. Take off in a parodic direction that utilizes your recollection but that places this material into totally inappropriate surroundings.

A recent viewing of director Federico Fellini's absorbing, self-absorbed 1963 film, *8½*, inspired such a parodic response from me. The film is about a Fellini-like director, who swarmed by sycophants and groupies, suffers agonies of indecision about what will be his next film and about his tangled personal life, all the while suffering heroically for Art. The film, in my opinion, is both magnificently parodic and unintentionally self-parodic. The *good* parody stems from the ambiguous parodic binding of multiple levels of reality—this keeps the viewer trapped in a confused maze that mirrors the confusion of Guido, the Fellini surrogate played by Marcello Mastroianni. The *good/bad* self-parody is a function of the film's over-the-top pretension, which despite self-protective layers of ironic mockery at Guido's expense, fails to absolve the enterprise from the campy grandiosity and silliness that licks all around the edges of the production.

And here is my own parodic response to the film (presented as a not-ready-for-prime-time writing exercise rather than a finished piece of work):

9:30

In LaWanda's surrealistic account of her shopping expedition at Kroger, time and the entire market seem to stand still as she, the narcissistic center of this spectacle, lords her way through the vegetable section, the simpering, fawning Kroger staff at her instant command and disposal, and with illimitable choices, she is engulfed by indecision, unable to decide between grotesque bunches of radishes, the *nouveau* sheen of acorn squash, or a gaggle of lewd zucchinis. Just as her earlier foray at Crate and Barrel emitted the metaphysical stench of crafty mall rats at play in their soulless suburban retreats, her 9:30 a.m. saunter through Kroger confirms all the *petit bourgeois* stereotypes about Ladies-Who-Market. We are privy to LaWanda's tangled reveries about baked beans, her conflicts with artichokes, and her anguished response to ratatouille. We learn that LaWanda must "get a grip" before she can come to terms with the orgasmic splendors of crockpot cooking. Her multifaceted diary entry reveals the strange inner life of a kitchen wunderkind, but, perhaps, it unwittingly reveals a deep-seated wish for instant, television commercial-style gratification, such as delivering one's culinary hopes and dreams over to reheated packages of frozen Tater Tots.

You can, of course, parodize any work that appeals to you, but I urge you to tackle pre-existing parodic art like *8½*. I'm convinced that the quickest and best way to learn the variations of the parodic technique is to choose juicy passages for practice from parodies that have already been written—and to adaptively parodize these examples into new contexts, such as what you did on your summer vacation or how you hope to become a Kardashian.

Of course, no one teaches this sort of imitative approach to writing anymore, because wonderful education pioneers like Jean-Jacques Rousseau and John Dewey and institutional black holes such as college and university education schools have freed school kids and schools in the United States from the burdens of rote learning, the acquisition of mere information, and the need for sanity.

Even so, the total eclipse of the approach to writing instruction that was once a universal standard in no way invalidates the ancient method's effectiveness or its practicality. So here is your homework. The succeeding chapters exemplify various parodic subtypes. With each,

1. Choose a passage that appeals to you and copy, copy, copy the passage until you get a feel for its style, its diction, its syntax, and its rhythm—and, if you desire to have what you've copied remain in your head, submit to the pain of actually memorizing it.
2. Parodize the parody. Again, take your selected passage and put it to new uses, like my response to the Fellini film. In other words, place the material in environs where it does not seem to belong. Once you get going, do the same with other excerpts from each parody in each chapter.

From this point forward, I am going to present for your target practice a series of twelve parodies, all devised by me, that exemplify the more accessible iterations of the parodic technique. In the chapters ahead, not all of the chief subiterations of parody will come into play. Instead of inclusivity, I will focus on those variations of the technique that are easiest to generate and to turn into finished works.

Thus I will introduce three little parodies dominated by disjunctive bangs; three that favor bunched binding; three that are typified by blended mimicry; and three that prominently feature blended mutations. Of these twelve parodies, nine are general parody spoofs, the type that is by far the most prevalent variety of short, humorous parodies published in this era, and only three of my exemplary parodies are permeated with mimicry which, again, is generally—and very mistakenly—cited by dictionaries, handbooks, and scholarly works as *the* defining feature of all parody.

After exemplifying ways to utilize parody for short bursts and comic performances, I will suggest in a final chapter how to use these weapons to create more sophisticated works in the great modernist and postmodernist formats that have nabbed top billing in the academically approved mainstream of twentieth- and twenty-first century writing. Such sophisticated parody is less fun to create or to read than strictly comic parodies, and the audiences for such work is shrinking (and probably taking down with it readership in general), but, hey, this is where big-league writing still resides.

Along with offering a dozen of my parodies and along with some commentary meant to help you forge similar parodies, I will include a few of the preliminary lists and *all* of the work sheets that have accompanied each of my twelve demos. The work sheets in the chapters ahead illuminate the processes of parodic construction. They strip each parody down to its core.

Those readers who feel ready to fly solo should approach these succeeding chapters as sample flights and sample flight plans. Maybe they'll provide you with a few ideas. Those readers who want to follow Plan B and to copy/parodize existing parodies should look to the exemplary parodies in these chapters for their material.

If my examples in the following chapters fail to please you and if you wish to look elsewhere for parodies to parodize, I heartily recommend Dwight Macdonald's *Parodies: An Anthology from Chaucer to Beerbohm—And After*. Conversely, I urge you to avoid the recent edition of *The Oxford Book of Parodies*, edited by John Gross. The latter includes a batch of mediocre and obscure parodies, and these are apparently the eccentric personal favorites of the late, beloved Mr. Gross, or perhaps they represent some last, quixotic effort on his part to showcase the halt, the blind, and the lame.

Finally, I know that there are lots of diagrams in this volume, an annoyance to some, but I think it will be helpful to add another one here. It's an outline of the chapter breakdown ahead:

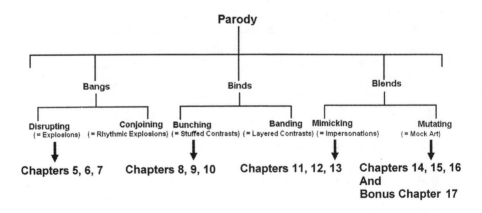

WHAT THIS BOOK WILL COVER

5.

Creating Disruptive Bangs I

Write what you know best is the enduring advice invariably laid on novices, a supremely obvious tip on a par with the admonition to keep breathing. As a budding parodist who takes this route, select raw and bloody chunks from your own miserable Life Story, the more grotesque and humiliating the better, because these are the choicest candidates for the parodic assembly line.

Here's a way to get started writing about a parodic version of yourself: any shrink will confirm that absolutely everyone has a psychiatric malady (which, given the slightest opportunity, the psychiatric community is committed to exacerbating), so the *Diagnostic and Statistical Manual* of mental plagues is an excellent resource for locating your particular personality disorder, and it will contain a concise list of your applicable symptoms, each of which can spur you to remember those hilarious occasions when you disgorged the hallmarks of your narcissism, your borderline or histrionic personality disorder, etc., in their fullest splendor. The time you shrieked and spat on Wilmer, for instance, when he attended to his dying wife's last rites rather than keeping a movie date with you, will leave your readers rollicking with laughter.

In my case, I had to make up a parodic autobio. After graduating from the Cincinnati College of Embalming, I spent the next fifty years of my life in a toilet I rented from the nonprofit purveyors of a soup kitchen in Bridgeport, Connecticut. During all those years, I never ventured out, cracking the door only to receive toilet paper and minestrone.

In the parodic example that follows, I invent a life worth writing about, but ultimately a parodic life story, partly real or utterly bogus, offers the opportunity (or excuse) for compiling a semi-related package of banging one-liners.

My preliminary list consists of potential joke material in a shorthand form, the meaning of which will become apparent in the completed parody:

PARODY	
TOPIC	**CONTRAST**
Fay Accompli	*auto de fe*
watermelon drippings	Seagram's VO
Elvis	Pocket Fisherman
Uvula GA	Dakota Territory
Baptist minister	Cue Ball
Pat Boone	April Hump

These scribblings led to my much more important second list, my work sheet:

Parody Work Sheet

TITLE

> "My Flaming Youth"

VARIATIONS

Bangs:	Binds:	Blends:
Yes ~~No~~	~~Yes~~ No	Yes ~~No~~
Major ~~Minor~~	~~Major~~ ~~Minor~~	~~Major~~ Minor

ITERATIVE DETAILS

STYLISTIC / NARRATIONAL CONTRASTS

> Primarily a mutated blend, a spoof, heavily nonsensical, of autobiographical essays, but the latter part of the essay is overlaid with blended mimicry of Hemingway's style and themes.

FORMAL / STRUCTURAL CONTRASTS

> The essay is dominated by disjunctive bangs, frequently consisting of a series of setups and punch lines, often in the form of one-liners.

OTHER CONTRASTS

> Some of the banging is not joke-based but is, instead, simply nonsensical: coherence gives way to incoherence or non sequiturs.

COMMENTS

> To some degree, there is an element of southern fried magic realism in this little narrative. It mixes elements of outlandish fantasy with dollops of white Dixieland in the 1950s and 1960s.

And with the parodic blueprint as a very real security blanket, I was able to flesh out what I hope is a reasonably disreputable parody:

My Flaming Youth

My shrink, Dr. Fay Accompli, has suggested that I dream up some sort of autobiographical record in order to "get a Life."

After obtaining a Life, I should, she opines, improve its overall quality by departing from it, preferably through a spectacular act of self-immolation within the confines of an automobile selected by Chrysler Corporation.

To hedge against the loss of fees from my marathon daily head-shrinking appointments, Dr. Fay has shrewdly acquired the reality-TV rights to my expected fiery end.

She might also deliver this footage (and headage) to *America's Funniest Home Videos* in exchange for "lotsa bucks" and a gold-trimmed Dodge Neon that will have such "custom car" features as jeweled mud flaps and a 1947 Kaiser ashtray.

What follows is my initial stab at Dr. Fay Accompli's project for me, a brief personal narrative about my coming of age, a whimsical first step towards my *auto de Fay.*

I remember my conception. It was a seminal event.

After that I remember very little until I was about thirteen. Then my mother, the Dowager Empress of China, married her second husband, a crouch potato, so named for the peculiar fetal position he assumed, day and night, as he snarfed a steady stream of watermelon drippings and Seagram's VO.

All this took place in the mid-1950s, at a time when American culture was being changed—changed utterly—by the emergence of Elvis Presley and Popeil's Pocket Fisherman.

My stepfather, Rex Tyrannosaurus, moved us to Uvula, Georgia, "The Dead Chicken Capital of the World."

Our little family included the aforementioned Rex and my mother, the Empressario, along with my brother, Hrothgar, and me—plus a potted pygmy pine tree that I, a budding druid, worshipped as a god.

I did not take our new home by storm, although I was a big chicken in my own right.

My chief accomplishment at the time consisted of having more exposed nerve endings than anyone in the region. I also reached the quarterfinals in the world finger-bowl placement competitions under the aegis of a grand master from Oberammergau. These qualities were not prized by a local populace, whose primary form of self-expression was the consumption of human flesh.

In short, Uvula back then was an extremely violent place. It was, though physically located in Georgia, still part of the Dakota Territory. All self-respecting citizens of Uvula were "hoods" who sported "duck-tail" haircuts—made from living ducks.

In Uvula, even the Baptist minister was a hood. That minister's real legal name was Cue Ball, and, if you did not attend the church of his choice, he would kill you.

Baptism in Cue Ball's church consisted of being bound, gagged, and pummeled by a former *gauleiter* in the Waffen-SS.

That man then dragged the initiate underwater for ten thousand meters behind the church's fiberglass ski boat, which had twin Mercury seventy-five-horsepower engines, jeweled mud flaps, and a 1917 Kaiser Wilhelm.

For the survivors of this preliminary ordeal, the ritual culminated in having your teeth knocked out by the church's lady orgasmist. Her name, as far as anyone knew, was Rabbit-Sniffer.

These missing teeth were normally replaced by religious *objets*, the sort of steel taps that are used to reinforce the immortal soles and heels of motorcycle boots. When a Baptist biker gentleman, to complete this digression, kisses his lady, known as a "hood ornament," these metal taps collide, raising sparks, a confluence that is invariably referred to as "scratching off."

After a succession of nurses and ballroom dance instructors, I was suddenly tossed into this Uvulesque environment like a delicate larva sinking into a cold lake full of bad basses.

I was beaten senseless to the rhythms of "Sh-Boom" and a host of Tin Pan Alley "crossover" hits, such as Pat Boone's rendition of the lovely "soul" ballad, "April Hump."

I also remember being bloodied to the accompaniment of some of the then-popular "cross-dressing" favorites, such as "Chantilly Lace and a Hairy Face" by Sam-the-Sham and The Transvestites.

I survived this ordeal, somehow, by creating my own songs, written under the aegis of Melvin "Sugar Booger" Rosenzweig, a country-western grand master and the first honky-tonk *shlemiel* to write a two-step tune about carpal tunnel syndrome.

Perhaps because he had been spotted with me, my Master, too, was beaten senseless. His nemesis turned out to be an out of control *oberammergauleiter* from the professional finger-bowling tour.

The aegis that I had been under was also beaten senseless, but fortunately it survived and hatched a brood of little aegises, removing that species from the endangered list.

Like so much great art, our work emerged from pain.

Perhaps, you remember some of my songs? I wrote "Blue Genes and Body Socks." I also scribbled "I Wanted to Let God in My Heart, But He Wouldn't Sign the Lease." And my personal favorite, "If Life Urinates on You, Make Pea Soup."

Sadly, the copyrights, the riches, and the fame, were stolen from me by the very same pygmy pine that I had worshipped with such heedless innocence. Otherwise, I, not that tree, would still be rolling in fertilizer, if not in clover.

I was country when country was cruel.

From these humble beginnings, I went on to create a place for myself as the town character and ritual scapegoat.

Even though my permissive parents were intrigued with the idea of my getting "stoned" at the quarry during the town's Mayan agricultural festivals, they decided to ship me away to a Southern boarding school. There, naturally, I learned, in an act of bitter, post-druid self-reclamation, to make boards.

All such schools in the region had a military format at the time of my incarceration. In my case, the choices narrowed down to Götterdämmerung Academy and Vlad the Impaler Institute. Both of these had parental appeal because, with their plutonium-manufacturing capabilities, the schools normally issued glowing report cards.

My parents chose Vlad the Impaler for its superior discipline. Although each of these august establishments required students to spit-shine their beds, Vlad the Impaler also demanded that students, rather than soil these shining pallets, sleep on pikes or, during periods of shortage, on rotting carp.

As with all such Southern institutions, the school's *raison d'être* was the deification of football "in order to promote violence in the home." With a grand old Southern rhetorical flourish, the headmaster referred to the non-football portion of the curriculum as "calendar-plugging year-wax."

In another installment, I will tell you about my days at Cheez Whiz University. I will write about my great friends Johnny Cake, Lou Soup, and Ardis Vark and how we sold the Mason Shoes and the *Grit* door to door.

I will tell you how, in the fall of the year, the cheez was always there, but we did not whiz anymore until the urologists circled us like sharks.

I will tell you how I was in another country and how the earth was prepared to move or, at least, to consider temporary relocation and how the shaven-headed Maria proved to be none other than Sam-the-Sham, of transvestial fame, who gave me the slip.

You will hear how I downed the carafes of kaolin at the Gritty Palace until the lady proctologist, Adrianna, said that we must say good-bye because being with me was mixing business with pleasure.

You will hear about my great love, Ms. Ann Thrope, and how my telling her story put thoughts of the Big Score into the head of my therapistol, Dr. Fay Accompli.

You will learn that Ann was good and straight and true until "the rich" and their "pilot fish," a one-eyed Portuguese bastard, exposed our bathtub ring at Schruns in the Vorarlberg.

Because of the shame and because she could no longer afford to attend fire sales, Ms. Ann Thrope wanted to be drenched in lighter fluid and set ablaze. So my life became all *nada* and *nada* plus a little extra *pues nada* because I realized finally that I could not hold a candle to her.

6.

Creating Disruptive Bangs II

A version of the example below originally appeared in *The Atlanta Journal* in the early 1980s. In short order, I produced a longer version, the one that appears here. The premise, then and now, is that the stock market is crazy and that nonsense art is the most adequate way to describe or respond to it. The piece was written many years before genuine, world-destroying insanity prevailed in the markets. Also, since I wrote the little parody, much has changed in this realm, but the more things change in the financial markets, the more things stay heedlessly the same.

My preliminary list simply amounted to a few jottings to get me going on the right path and to exemplify the all-out anarchy I wanted to capture:

PARODY	
TOPIC	**CONTRAST**
Stock Market	**Soup Fermentation**
Definition	**tsetse, tsunami, Tsunday, tsetse offensive**
stock brokers	**snow cones, asbestos installing**
cold calls	**let Prince Albert out of can**
IPOs	**I. P. Freelys**

Again, most of these notes are in a sort of shorthand that made sense just to me— and that material only becomes slightly more coherent in the non-sense of the story proper. But, as a preliminary list is supposed to do, this one sets up a pattern.

With the list in hand, I fashioned this parodic blueprint:

Parody Work Sheet

TITLE

> "Market Zen, Or, The Wages of Zen Is Death"

VARIATIONS

Bangs: Yes ~~No~~ Major ~~Minor~~	Binds: ~~Yes~~ No ~~Major Minor~~	Blends: Yes ~~No~~ ~~Major~~ Minor

ITERATIVE DETAILS
STYLISTIC / NARRATIONAL CONTRASTS

> A plain vanilla general parody spoof bordering upon purely anarchic nonsense, but here and there the narration veers into satiric condemnation of Wall Street excess.

FORMAL / STRUCTURAL CONTRASTS

> The essay depends almost entirely on disjunctive banging--a series of setups and punch lines.

OTHER CONTRASTS

> Scattered throughout are a few bits of wordplay (such as "scalpel" and "scalp, pal").

COMMENTS

> There is, finally, something of a clash between the overall playful tone and the glimmers of seriousness, the net effect of which is an evasive quality and an abrupt, bathetic ending.

This is the parody that has emerged:

MARKET ZEN, OR, THE WAGES OF ZEN IS DEATH

You can lose your organs and your harmonica in the stock market, but let's face it: the experience provides a much jazzier high than those associated with the proceedings, say, of the Thirteenth Congress on Glandular Irregularities and Soup Fermentation.

If you're ready to accept that proposition, then I'm ready to sell you on stocks. What are they? Well, most kinds of stocks, along with pillories, dunking platforms, and branding irons, are Puritan-era torture devices.

Torture is a recurring motif in this kind of discussion because becoming truly familiar with the stock market is like becoming especially intimate with a scalpel, and because it's your scalp, pal.

Frankly, the stock market will only begin to make sense if you compare its strange, unexpected rising and falling movements to the crazed leaping dances of hallucinated Japanese sushi chefs. Perhaps, the chefs' minds (or the market's) have been deranged by a plague of swarming tsetse flies washed up by a tsunami one fateful Tsunday afternoon.

Perhaps, also, the undulating movements of the market, like those of the sushi chefs, are mere mirrors of the manic-depressive brain waves of that greatest of all sushi chefs, the sexually insatiable and eternally potent, "Stake"Teriyaki.

Perhaps, finally, the random dance of the stock market is, like life itself, a high-wire trampoline act performed without a *netsuke* and leaving us all victimized by sudden tsetse offensives.

If you have nothing more important to do than to read this kind of clap-trap, then you have time to "play" the market. If so, hurry up and buy some stocks to cling to in the night—before they run out of them or before their prices simply evaporate.

To get yours (literally and figuratively), you'll have to buy stocks from some kind of investment firm. These offer ever-wider ranges of services through their crooked salespeople. Such services now include snow cones, same-day asbestos installation and removal, and the hot-wiring of maiden aunts.

Of course, investment firms don't want their sales folk to get so distracted by all these products that they lose sight of their primary task, which is to call elderly widows late at night to tell them to let Prince Albert out of the can.

Sometimes these same salespeople cold call late at night when *you* are on the can and tell you about an upcoming, first-ever issuance of some company's stock, one of those famous Initial Pubic Offerings. These are also called "IPOs" and are sometimes known as "I. P. Freelys."

IPOs are tricky because a company with stock that is about to be offered to the public for the very first time will sometimes kick and scream and act skittish about it, but inevitably the company relents if the investment firm promises to be very gentle and not to tell anyone afterward. This compact between a company and the underwriters who bring the stock to market is known as "white water canoeing" or "The Wilmot Proviso."

For its part, an underwriting firm helps the company "cook its books" while attempting to churn up interest in the company's stock until a very murky and toxic broth has been produced. These book-cooking manipulations, in the fight to see who can produce the biggest "whoppers," often push a company close to civil war, pitting broth against brother.

After the stock has been forcibly transferred into public hands at hospital intensive care units, bus station waiting rooms, and fast organ donation franchises, the victims of these transactions may often seek to avoid disgrace by auctioning off their stock to someone else or by simply purging it with laxatives.

Auction services are performed by organizations called "shock exchanges." These may be "real" physical entities, such as the New York Shock Exchange, a bizarre bazaar that somehow blends the worst features of *The Arabian Nights* and Jiffy Lube. Or an exchange may be nothing more than a computer network such as NASDAQ, which is an electronic game supplied by Nintendo.

The auction process on the New York Shock Exchange is controlled by saintly dwarfettes called "specialists" who subspecialize in full-contact karate and whining.

On NASDAQ, all the real action is in the hands of "day traders," who gain or lose trillions of dollars instantly and endlessly until their mommies tell them to come home and clean up their rooms. The smartest kids never go home at all. They have invented, out of thin air, ticking bombs called *derivatives*, and because no one understands them, the kids can make trillion-dollar bets with no money down and collect billion-dollar fees with no supervision except that from stray truant officers or dog catchers.

Derivatives were designed originally to blow up Cleveland, but as the "engineering" has improved, derivatives can now provide financial incontinence to whole continents.

And so, Mom-and-Pop, as the new millennium enters and human prosperity draws to an end, you could do worse than finding and marrying yourself to a ripe, willing boy or girl stock or derivative and, as your gender preferences dictate, pressing your apocalypse to theirs.

Other players who also want to court Armageddon can advance their self-destruction by heeding a securities brokerage firm's commission-driven "strong buy-buy-buy" and "very strong buy-buy-buy" stock purchase recommendations. These recommendations alternate every day at sunup and sundown.

A securities firm, by the way, will never recommend that you sell your shares— "because that might piss off Freddy." Freddy is Steve's cousin by marriage.

Securities firms are able to offer an endless stream of rotten advice because they hire hordes of analysts, who are also known as "anal cysts." These worthy souls "follow" various companies that have issued stock, hoping that some of these companies will take pity on them, set them up in a Park Avenue co-op, and keep them in whorish splendor.

Analysts also make funny noises and gestures when they've captured a stock's attention. The written records of these noise-fests are known as "research reports," but sometimes these documents are merely encoded guides to physically harmful varieties of tantric sex.

Securities analysts are of two sorts.

"Fundamental analysts" temper absurd prognoses about a company's future with lots of accounting nonsense after they have taken a company's temperature the old-fashioned way. That's where the "fundament" part comes in, as anyone who remembers his or her grammar school humor will have already guessed.

Fundamental analysts also do light tailoring and one-hour Martinizing.

"Technical analysts," on the other hand, base their mumbo-jumbo on their "reading" of charts that show how much a stock's price went up or down, how much of the stock was bought and sold, and how many evil demons and spirits were in the vicinity at the time.

To summarize all this and to draw a final bleed on the nature of stocks, we need only recall what J. P. "Chuck" Morgan, that greatest of all financiers, said about the future of his investments: "They will continue to up-Chuck," he bellowed.

7.

Creating Disruptive Bangs III

At this point, it seems unnecessary to keep printing all the entries I made in the preliminary lists that preceded each of my parodies. The purpose of these lists should by now be more than evident: the method, once explained, hardly requires repetition (and my laundry list shorthand can be mystifying and tends to remain so until the meaning becomes clear in the parody proper).

Therefore, in succeeding chapters, I will post only those preliminary jottings that inspired, in epiphanic moments, the parodies that grew from them or those initial notions that may help, if need be, explain the rationale behind an upcoming parody. So, for the most part, I will offer in each of the remaining chapters only (a) a bit of commentary; (b) my blueprint; and (c) a parodic example.

There is one aspect of preliminary lists, though, that remains to be mentioned. They can be a useful resource for generating one-liners, an essential, if elementary, ingredient of parodic banging.

Normally, when creating a preliminary list, I first supply a topic and then hunt for one that contrasts with it. But when attempting to scrounge up one-liners, I may reverse the process and begin my search by first seeking explosive material—in other words, punch lines—and then I search for topics, contrasting setups to magnify the power of the unexpected punch lines.

For example, as proof that I am not very inventive (or funny) and that my mind has not evolved much beyond schoolyard gutters, I stumbled on the term *schadenfreude*, which English has borrowed from German and which actually means pleasure in the misfortune of others. With my polymorphously perverse sensibility, I could instantly discern that the word could also be perceived as fractured English, its message extrapolated as "shat-in-[Sigmund] Freud." Here, then, was a likely punch line awaiting only an innocent-seeming setup to disclose the basis of its cheap scatological kick:

PARODY	
TOPIC	**CONTRAST**
?????	*schadenfreude*

After, fumbling a bit, I decided that the phrase "psychiatric diarrhea" had emerged as a suitable joke-establishing mechanism, and, with it, the joke can be deployed in various kinds of syntactical arrangements, the simplest of which is this preliminary listing:

PARODY	
TOPIC	**CONTRAST**
Q: Define psychiatric diarrhea	A: *Schadenfreude*

These joke-chasing exercises, like the doddering TV show *Jeopardy*, which spits out answers to which the contestants must supply the questions, inspired my idea for a parodic spoof (that remains unwritten and is yours for the taking). The spoof might be called something like "'Punch Line' Pete," and it would be about a stand-up comic who speaks only in punch lines to which the people in his life, who want or need intelligible dealings with him, must supply the setups.

The parody that follows deals with televised material that is far more fetid than *Jeopardy* during its most embarassing moments. And I've probably lost at least part of a bet about the parody that I'd made with myself at the time of its writing: I bet that the parody could, somehow, withstand its topicality and scads of references that would surely become dated, if not wholly forgotten. I was worried about all this, and I mentioned such concerns in the blueprint that was produced well before the parody's final draft. At the time, I wrote, "This is a chancy piece of writing in that it parodizes people, places, and things that are potentially headed for oblivion. The bet has to be that the material will stand alone without the references."

Well, many of the people, places, and things mentioned in the parody have certainly reverted to the nothingness from whence they sprang. But, of more importance, my subject, the raw tastelessness of network television in the 1970s, has been supplanted by the then-undreamed of levels of cultural barbarism that putrefy hundreds of channels on the tube today, so it's questionable that my bang-ridden little parody still has much kick.

My best hope for this parody is that it has some claim on a reader's attention because of a nostalgia factor and because of the reemergence of this goop on cable and DVDs. Unfortunately, this 1970s TV crap continues to survive and is endlessly repeated on *Nickelodeon* and other channels.

My blueprint for my '70s TV parody follows:

Parody Work Sheet

TITLE

> "Tube Nostalgia--The Soaring 70s"

VARIATIONS

Bangs:	Binds:	Blends:
Yes ~~No~~	~~Yes~~ No	Yes ~~No~~
Major ~~Minor~~	~~Major~~ ~~Minor~~	Major ~~Minor~~

ITERATIVE DETAILS

STYLISTIC / NARRATIONAL CONTRASTS

> Fizzy-but-grating showbizzy mock form stylistics throughout.
> The narration produces a mutated blend, but it traipses into
> some mimicry (eg. the Anka song & the Bareass/Barris interview).

FORMAL / STRUCTURAL CONTRASTS

> Each of the little vignettes climaxes, rather, anti-climaxes with a
> parodic bang. Some are interspersed with one-liner bangs, but
> others simply build to a mini-explosion of one sort or another.

OTHER CONTRASTS

> Real 1970s players are identified either by name or by mimicked
> name (eg. Jerry La Famine/Jerry Della Femina). After the I.D.s
> warped versions of these folks's 1970s output follows.

COMMENTS

> This is a chancy piece of writing in that it parodizes people,
> places, and things potentially headed for oblivion. The bet has to
> be that the material will stand alone without the references.

And here is the parody:

Tube Nostalgia—the Soaring '70s

Remember *Spin and Marty McLuhan*? They were a boffo hubby-n-wife team in 1973, but they got scuttled by a prime-time overload of spin-offs.

Marty went on to become a Media Guru with that fab gimmick of his about how each medium relates meaningfully to your bod. Books are like eyes, and the Tube Itself is, yes, Action Central, the spinal cord.

For a while, every Media Czar slept a little easier knowing that at the base of his network he was protected by Don Coccyx. But that's all kaput now. Spin says her life went into "a rinse cycle," and before he died, poor Marty was blown out of the Media Rink, Talk Show Division, by a new, designated Canadian guest, former hockey great, *Bernie "Boom-Boom" Geoffrion*.

We like to remember Marty back when he was on a roll. The time, for instance, when Science Biggie *Carl Sagan* told him that the whole ever-loving universe premiered with a humongous Big Bang blast that is still pulling everything apart.

For Non-Science Biggies, this sort of info would have been strictly a sleeping pill, but not after a pro like Marty had flavored it with seven herbs and spices. Soon Marty was pulling down ten figs per gig, and he radicalized a whole new generation of media groupies.

It was beautiful stuff. All about the Nuclear Family being slowly stretched into ion dots and how the flickering ion image of *Merv Griffin* on your TV screen represents the final, most advanced stage of human evolution.

Our favorite year? Maybe it was 1977, with that fierce, pitched battle for the 8:00 p.m. Monday time slot.

From CBS (and *Freddy Silverman*'s Blue Period) came *Wayne Newton* as that lovable old racist ice cream peddler in *Good Humor Honkie*. The motivation for his hilarious bigotry was "popsicle sell anemia."

The competition got fierce when ABC brought in *Roone Arledge*, who promptly mined Freddy's Rose Period with a series about a topless, top-spinning lady tennis pro. Each show combined a "thrill of victory" tennis match with an "agony of defeat" earthquake, and the irresistible title for this shaky package was *The San Andreas Double Fault*.

NBC, of course, took the biggest gamble and the biggest fall by tapping Freddy's startling Cubist Period. *Sandy Duncan* was cast as an ashtray in *My Car, the Mother* until the series was canceled by executive fiat.

Then, when no clear winner emerged from the Monday night Nielsens, the three networks came out of the closet and aired the same series with virtually the same script at the same time. But with different stars, naturally. *Farrah Fawcett Majors* on CBS, *Barbara Eden* on ABC, and *Charo* on NBC—all played *Julia*

"Jiggles" Child in that series about the battle for gourmet rights, *Brie at Last! Thank God Almighty, Brie at Last!*

Nothing about those shows was canned but the laughter.

Our candidate for the most surprising loser of the decade has to be *The Manson Family* back in 1976. ABC claimed that the show just wasn't mellow enough, and that injection of 1930s-style nostalgia didn't cut it either.

"Spanky" McFarland was miscast as the Spahn Ranch, and there were scads of controversy about the show's weepy intro, "Remember *Charlie Manson*? When times were hard, he put kids back to work."

In the last few episodes, the producers tried to jack up the series with a religious angle. Spanky was shifted to the role of *San Juan de la Cruz*, and *Billy Graham* was booked to play Los Angeles. The new intro explained the revamped theme: "In my Father's house there are many Mansons." But, hey, nothing seemed to cut the mustard.

Remember, there was a little, bitty economic depression back in 1974, but how could we have been downhearted during this period, what with all those fabulous creative thoughts that emerged about the human foot?

Mr. Mad Ave Himself, *Jerry La Famine*, jerked us out of our feetal position. He "broke down all the barriers between commercials and commercial programming" in the process of packaging a series that simply reeked with culture while shuffling through the virtues of Odor Eater foot pads and allied products like corn plasters and crust repellent.

As feet would have it, the first show in *FootNotes to U.S. History* dealt with the rivalry between *George* ("First in War and First in Feet") *Washington* and the Polish *General Koshoesko*, who was reported to have had the most enormous brogans on the continent.

The series strolled down Memory Lane with shows on foot culture heroes like *Paul Bunion* and *Edgar Allan Toe.*

Eventually, as Jerry put it, "the thing became some kind of a fetish," and the series concluded with the European Athlete's Foot Epidemic of 1919.

The new world came to the rescue of the old as *"Shoeless Joe" Jackson* and other members of the *Chicago "Black Sox"* baseball team turkey trotted onto the shores of France with the stirring pronouncement, *"Le Feet* we are here!"

Who'd have thought you could top a series like that, but Jerry did it by nailing down a personal services contract with *Albert Speer*, Hitler's favorite stand-up architect and Slave Master.

Then Jerry and his pal, that Sweet-and-Sour Kraut, commanded holocaust fees for Al's commercial monologues.

Here's a snatch from one of the more memorable routines: "Although I willingly embrace the condemnation of Eternity for sending a few, perhaps, no more than two million forced laborers to their deaths, I must patiently add that these policies were formulated near the end of the war by subordinates who kept me uninformed and by that madman, *Adolf Hitler*, who held me mesmerized for fifteen years, rendering me blind to his faults because of our shared interests in preventing eruptions of the skin.

"The private Hitler I once worshipped craved *lebensraum* all right—but only for clogged pores at the expense of alien goobs and blotches."

The next step, when the price was right, was the Speermint Gum campaign, which came at a time when Al and Jerry could afford to be chewsy. Then it was on to cereals (Speerios) because Al said he loved promoting perishables.

Honestly, we were the dopes who thought that Jerry had made his ultimate statement in the early 1970s when he pioneered the Feminine Hygiene Movement and brainstormed the campaign theme song, "Our Love Is Here to Spray."

For some of us, the whole decade belongs to the King of the Telethons and one of our very favorite Geniuses, *Jerry Lewis*.

What you probably don't know is that, back in 1978, he tried to grab even more Tube Exposure for his Showbiz Heart of Gold. He planned, as he said, "to squeeze some art from dying old farts."

But the greedy Network Cabals were telethoned out. They killed *Jazzy Jerryatrics* before Our Man had a chance to get those near-comatose old buzzards rockin' and boppin.'

Paul Anka, natch, had even kicked in another classic theme song for this stillborn *Cootenanny*:

> When your life isn't sweet,
> and disease rots your feet,
> and you can't move your arm,
> and you ain't got no charm,
> then it isn't too soon
> to become a balloon.
> Yes, we'll wave as you pass
> once they've filled you with gas
> 'cause it's up, up with people.
> Get them up there today.
> Up, up with people
> in the U. S. of A.

From *"Chunky" Bareass*, as usual, came the climactic shows of the decade. In 1979, remember, he outflanked his own blockbusters with *The God Dating Gong Game*.

Was God really on these shows? so many of us wondered. "You got that right, buckaroos," Chunky told us. "Because, jeez, there's a little bit of God in everybody, so we didn't have to scout around much.

"It's like everything is beautiful, and everyone is God in his own way.

"It's the God Module in the Cats we scraped out of the gutter and off the wall that we put on the air.

"Once they got on the show, it was like their gig all the way.

"They could do a little faith healing, a little belly dancing, make a few animal noises, or whatever.

"The losers got gonged back to the gutter.

"The winner was crowned King of Kings. Then it was like off to Vegas for a weekend with a broad who could turn his water to wine."

How did Chunky know that this would "play in Peoria," we wanted to know. What made him sure that Mr. and Mrs. J. Q. Public wouldn't think that the show was maybe a little tasteless?

"Listen," Chunky told us, "I love those people out there. Don't you forget it—the American Public is truly God.

"And remember this, too: nobody ever went broke underestimating the taste of God."

8.

Creating Bunched Binds I

Bunched binds can be understood as "parodic conceits," meaning extended anti-metaphors (as opposed to the normal definition of "conceits" as elaborate metaphors). Creators of the latter strive to find unity and identity in far-fetched comparisons while parodists forge bonds that are meant to remain outlandish, inappropriate, and/or impossible. But, if a parodic conceit is successful, its preposterous components can seem at once both radically separate and very married—a multistable illusion like the rabbit/duck drawing. For a parodist, the happiest of circumstances is to chance on an unlikely combination that is striking, hilariously unsuitable or uncongenial, and that can be extended indefinitely throughout a literary application.

The first parodies, for instance—rather, the first to be identified by Aristotle over 2,000 years ago—were such extended parodic conceits. Mock epics and comic epics are parodies that bind heroic or epic conventions to egregiously nonheroic, nonepic subject matter.

In comic epics and in many other instances of parodic binding, the extended material is intermingled and mixed together in a helter-skelter fashion. Hence my terminology "bunched binding."

The distinction between bunched binding and a related subset of iterations that I call "banded binding" is that, in the latter, separate, contrasting levels of narrational, structural, or plot material are maintained consistently as parallel alternatives but are played against one another in a confusing, ambiguous, and multistable manner. Stories-within-stories that are contradictory and other ambiguous alternatives nested within a work of art are typical mainstays.

The border between bunched and banded binding, however, is not always entirely clear-cut. For instance, a highly formal mock epic, Alexander Pope's *The Rape of the Lock*, rigorously maintains a clear separation between an epic manner of poetic narration and a radically nonepic story line, creating and upholding contrasting levels in the process. As a result, such a work sits on a cusp at the point of intersection between bunched and banded binding.

Banded binding, as I mentioned in the first chapter, is typically utilized in serious or semi-serious comedies, such as those by playwrights Luigi Pirandello and Tom Stoppard or in some of the films of Woody Allen and others. At this point, however, I will cease further mention of banded binding and stick, as promised, with their bunched relations, which are, no surprise, easier to write and less likely to contain wads of heavy philosophical goulash.

For various reasons, I'm a fan of both country and western music and of the art and history of imperial China. In a serendipitous moment years ago, it suddenly occurred to me that a parodic binding of the two would be a winningly bizarre combination:

PARODY	
TOPIC	CONTRAST
Imperial China	The Grand Ole Opry

Both of these subject areas have warehouses brimming with conventions— elaborate and formal in the traditions of old China and wholly informal and quite often oozingly sentimental in the case of the sometimes hokey traditions of the Opry. Country music songs, like Chinese literature and painting, can be filed neatly into genres and subgenres containing similar material. Such material is generally worthy of serious consideration in the case of Chinese culture but essentially less so in terms of the bar songs, prison songs, adultery songs, and the like that populate the C&W generic spectrum. But, of course, the point is that, despite some fortuitously accidental similarities, the contrast between imperial Chinese civilization and the saccharine, show-bizzy world of country music couldn't be more stark or more extreme.

Happily, I was aware of a wonderful word, *chinoiserie*, that begged to be a part of my theme-bearing title. *Chinoiserie*, you may recall, means Western ideas about the Orient, as expressed in a sometimes very odd, hybrid fashion in art or in decorative objects. Not only does the term imply a weird mingling of East and West, but the pronunciation of the last syllable in *chinoiserie* sounds enough like *Opry* to cement at least an aural comic connection.

I wrote this parody in the late 1970s, at which time there was already a distinction between "hard country," the original, musically primitive, and often mournfully wailing sound that purists claimed was the only true kind of country music, and "soft country," a far smoother sound, typically, with a full orchestra, that was designed to appeal to pop music fans as well as to the lovers of the Opry.

Soft country has won, and the crossover has succeeded so well that it is often very difficult to distinguish country from pop. My parody was written when hard country music and its icons were still more or less the distinguishing, if not commanding, entities in this world, and so I guess my parody has become a primitive artifact, like hard country itself.

Parody Work Sheet

TITLE

> "The Grand Ole Chinoiserie Newsletter"

VARIATIONS

Bangs:	Binds:	Blends:
Yes ~~No~~	Yes ~~No~~	Yes ~~No~~
Major ~~Minor~~	Major ~~Minor~~	Major ~~Minor~~

ITERATIVE DETAILS

STYLISTIC / NARRATIONAL CONTRASTS

> Style = reflexive Babbitry, meaning noxious, insincere folksiness with occasional flights of reflexive formality. Specific parody of country star names, song titles, and snatches of songs.

FORMAL / STRUCTURAL CONTRASTS

> A work of bunched binding stemming from the delusion that the traditions of American country music and Imperial Chinese culture are one and the same.

OTHER CONTRASTS

> There is a parade of disruptive bangs particularly in the anti-climactic verse, in the Sino-American star names, and in the numerous puns such as "New York Foos."

COMMENTS

> Despite elements of specific parody, this little fiction is a work of bunched binding and a general parody spoof.

Folks in Music City are predicting imminent stardom for *Da Na Fa Go*, the Cathay Cowgirl. Da Na started pumping out her special brand of yellow soul music back in the days when she hawked Tupperware *jui-i* scepters to pig-faced foreigners and to touring pink-necked peasants in the steaming back alleys of Gatlinburg.

Da Na hit the big time when she offended the Jesuits (alien priests who were allowed to live in Murfreesboro as long as they wound the Emperor's clocks). Our little Honky-Tonk Angel rocked and shocked them with "I Wanna Play Roadhouse":

> A scholar whose rounds are through
> dreams of *Lao Tzu*,
> but a monk who can burn some gas
> should head for the Hanku Pass.
> There at HoJo's 28,
> ringed by Interstate 8,
> he'll find that my girlish favors
> explode in thirty flavors
> and batter his monkish vows
> till he throws in the *Tao*.

Da Na prepared for this triumph by spending thirty flavorful minutes learning guitar chords and an equal amount of time practicing calligraphy on the sacred, white tiles of public toilets.

Still, friends say she'd have socked it to 'em sooner if she'd decided to follow in the footsteps of *Da Lee Pai-ton* and to sing of truck stops, go-go bars, and opium dens. Instead, Da Na chose a minor master and spent a lurid apprenticeship wailing about the least succulent aspects of "Dear Chun" letters, adultery, and divorce.

And speaking of bad trips, *Min Nei Pearl* says, "Never again, Doodlebug!" about touring the provinces. She had to yodel the names of the Eight Immortals at every whistle-stop and Grinder's Switch, Min Nei told us. And, she said, "I froze my noogies off at VFW posts from here to Hunan singing 'The Whampoa Cannonball' while popping out naked from giant mounds of bean curd."

What can we say about the late *Wei-lon Chen Nin?* It's true that he flirted with Taiwan Alley and the pop charts (remember, he wrote "It Was Just One of Those Mings"). But Wei-lon brought it all back home when he stomped out the juice and savored the whine of "Thank God I'm a Kwang-si Boy":

> When I'm on stage they don't pop no pills,
> and the acupunctures stop.
> I cure folks' ills with a big old grin
> and sentimental slop.

Wei-lon, we think, would still be out there slopping away—if he hadn't whizzed on the Emperor's miniature automobile graveyards in the Gardens of Wu Liang.

There aren't many tears in the life of *Chun Yi Cash*'s lovely wife, *Sun Myung June*. She gets her grins spending money on filmy, Day-of-the-Week undergarments by *Frederick of Haikow*. Or June finds "boss" duds for Chun Yi—like that beautiful simulated-velveteen tapestry robe of his (it depicts the great *Tex Woo Ta* being welcomed into Hillbilly Heaven by *Chek* and *Bao-bei*, the martyred brother Emperors of the *Old Cho Dynasty*).

June, a Confucian duty-freak like her husband, says that her life would be "a whole lot more perfect" if only novice singers didn't try to bribe their way into Cash performances by turning *twiks*, or "special services," for powerful Mandarin officials. But she adds, philosophically, "No twikee, no watchee."

Happy news. *Genghis Kristofferson* has finally lived down his reputation as a scholar-type expert on the Yuan Dynasty. To clear the air, Genghis trashed his old teachers and issued a disclaimer ("The Yuan," he said, "make me drowsy"). Now, apart from *Moo Ha Gud*, nobody in the industry has more top-quality felony convictions than Genghis, and for his part, Genghis thinks his songs are better than Moo's.

At the moment, Genghis is scrambling the eggheads with his latest smash, "Me in My TR-3":

> Near the end of my years
> I have found peace
> at the dirt tracks of Shensi.
> Soon I shall be free
> from this Life's Turning Wheel.
> In other lives, I would hope to be
> the hardest of Hard Chargers,
> a battery, with my twelve volts attached
> to Hertz Shifters, solid lifters,
> and jeweled mud-flaps.

More kudos. Congrats to *"Spade" Coolie* for winning the "Elks' Year of the Greased Pig Sing-Off" up at the Temple of the Glad Hand in Tullahoma. Spade (can you dig it?) hit them with his own original composition, "The Homefolks Think I'm Big in Heilungkiang":

> Far from my mountain home,
> I sink in pools of beer.
> As carp collide,
> I vomit forth my night-shift rage.

In the wake of this ditty, Spade advanced in rank from *Tah-drih* to *Chin-shih* musician. He earned a one-night, one-set stand at the Ri-mein Pavilion, and he landed the Prefecture of Soddy-Daisy.

But let's face it, the "Spades" don't usually make it in country music. There's got to be a fine sense of timing in a real star's career. Like the way the famous *Lo-Lin* first roared out of a canebrake and capitalized on her lowly origins with "I'm Proud to Be a Bird Breeder's Daughter":

> There just ain't no stopping
> this girl with bird droppings.

She sang, concluding with the declaration,

> I can bend, but I canebrake.

Lo Lin caught the right ears and caked the right brains with her message, and she glided into fame with her next biggie, "Stand by Your Mandarin."

From there it should have been easy, but Lo Lin let it be known that she *was not* having an affair with *Khan Wei Twi-ti*, that she *was* mother to fifteen healthy, legitimate children, and that she *was* happily married to *Moo Ni*, a toothless, one-eyed bootlegger of ginseng root.

This puerile conventionality was too much for the public to bear, and Lo Lin would have been deposited back in the bird secretions had she not tried to clear, in a rickshaw powered by a big Harley engine, both a mound in Monteagle and a pyramid formed by Moo Ni and the kiddies.

Owing to this rather messy public failure, her fame is secure, and the late Lo Lin leaves behind a legend and a puzzling pearl of a couplet:

> You ain't *Yin* enough
> to get my *Yang*.

Lo Lin was a great one, but, though the story is old and mildewy, when they made *Hun Wi-yums*, they formed the mold. Before this raunchy devil stormed the Great Wall of Gallatin and entered the town, Nashville audiences had revered such pallid religious songs as "I'll Cling to the Old, Rugged Swastika," and "We Need a Whole Lot More of Buddha and a Lot Less Egg Roll."

With a single lyric, Wi-yums reinterpreted the will of the gods and redirected the energies of country music:

> I don't want to mess up my life,
> but the gods I'm told love change and strife.

So, by gum, *I-Ching-o*, since they do,
I'll give 'em fightin', whorin', and self-pity too.

He also unleashed a sense of pride in his country's heritage:

The Yangtze Gorge is gorgeous.
That foam and muck beats all.
But they ain't got no souvenirs
like fuzzy dice from Ruby Falls.

Hun, in short, was that rarest of artists, one who speaks for a whole people:

I have a dream:
the night birds sing,
and evening bells at Lake Tung-ting
extol us local men,
our wisdom and our skin,
on nights that we lynch uppity whites
and burn some logs under running dogs,
whose views and hues are not pure yellow,
them New York Foos
like Rockefeller.

This running doggerel propelled Hun into a Command Performance, the rarest of honors, at the Emperor's palace in Wuhsien. There Hun was canonized by Imperial Rescript long before that terrible dawn when he consumed four gallons of antifreeze and the *famille verte* porcelain disks that studded his pickup truck.

As his cooling system was heating up, Hun explained the secret of his fame. "The Road to Excess," he said, "leads to the Palace of Wuhsien."

And that's it, the key to Hillbilly Heaven and to Country Music Sainthood—via self-annihilating depravity, a performer can spiral downward through deepening levels of sin, becoming at last the holiest of holy men, a good ole zonked-out Bodhisattva surrounded by a gaggle of good ole boy disciples at Tootsie's Lotus Lounge.

9.

Creating Bunched Binds II

A seemingly infantile sort of pairing—*hunger* and *Hungary*—inspired the following parody. At first glance, this combination, rather than representing an instance of parodic contrasts, might have appeared to be a concise factual summary of Cold War Soviet Bloc conditions in 1977 when the parody was published. However, what I had in mind was a thoroughgoing contrast:

PARODY	
TOPIC	**CONTRAST**
Hungary	All-consuming hunger

In fact, so omnivorous and cosmic is the hunger I ascribe to Hungarians that what begins as a parodic conceit evolves into a parodic "system." The latter term has been defined by the great Argentine parodist, Jorge Luis Borges, as "the subordination of all aspects of the universe to one of those aspects—any one of them." A system, also known as a "hobbyhorse" or simply as a psychotic obsession, is what becomes of plain vanilla parodic conceits when they become cancerous and turn into the artistic equivalent of kudzu.

A few years ago, parodic hoaxster Sacha Baron Cohen invented a character, Borat, for TV and film. Borat, although allegedly from Kazakhstan, speaks broken English in a manner resembling my faux Hungarian narrator. I'm sure Cohen does this sort of thing much better than I, but I have the satisfaction of having stumbled on this dubious format before him (but not before S. J. Perelman, as my blueprint acknowledged at the time).

Parody Work Sheet

TITLE

> "Hunger in Hungary"

VARIATIONS

Bangs:	Binds:	Blends:
Yes ~~No~~	Yes ~~No~~	Yes ~~No~~
Major ~~Minor~~	Major ~~Minor~~	Major ~~Minor~~

ITERATIVE DETAILS

STYLISTIC / NARRATIONAL CONTRASTS

> A mutated blend in faux Hungarian accented English replete with fractured grammar, syntax, and diction. While this goulash may seem like amateurish homage to S. J. Perelman, the language was actually inspired by some Hungarian industrial brochures I found.

FORMAL / STRUCTURAL CONTRASTS

> The bunched binding that orchestrates this work is based upon the punning conceit that Hungarians are hungry.

OTHER CONTRASTS

> There is constant disruptive parodic banging in the form of crude, pig bladder humor and far-fetched or gratingly obvious puns.

COMMENTS

> A general parody spoof, but, at the same time, a parodic *system* that subordinates all aspects of the universe to an obsession with food.

HUNGER IN HUNGARY

PEST, 1953—Always it is good to pour into Szekszard. We find a thoroughfare with one part turf and three parts creamy concrete. We blend with a crowd as thick as the mock meat paste from the Factory for Stretched Meat Zamat. And everywhere people are stirring in their attractive wrappers while their excellent water retention is as reliable as canned goods.

The autumn throbs as soft always tender Gyulai sausages contract in the frosted air. It is a time to dream of cryocentration, the water-removing technique that delivers apricots like tiny, always-wrinkled cannon balls. Autumn is mysterious as a woman, red-brown and dripping with ice splinters shaped like sweet Magyar salamanders in a savory local sauce or popular gravy.

While the temperature drops, the blood rises. The Hungarian man knows that autumn is the season to take a woman, to drag her quivering into corners, and to conquer her with news that Hungarian butter is never off-color and always free from off-odor.

Then the maiden will melt in the fall like Kashkeval, the white cheese from sheep milk. Perhaps she should be peeled like the cheese type Emmenthal, or she may be as easy as the Balaton spread.

If the need arises, the young man will perform experiments as varying as those at the Hungarian Dairying Institute. And always he is secure in knowing that if his woman has lost her flavor, she will be destroyed.

Before the winter rains is clearly the best of time to visit rural areas if the roads have not been eaten. There, fun begins with pigs. Preceding the happy slaughter festivities is certainly a game to always tease the animals with a traditional song, "If You So Damn Smart, Why You Not Pig Shot?" And there are laughter jokes to split the belly: "Difference between pig and Bulgarian is less tasty bristles and boiling time with pig." The butchered animal becomes pig salt, pig bread, and pig wine, in a cooking-converting performance that is surely pigturesque.

And soon it will be time to enter a period of lusty mourning for Hungarians overcome by chunks of boiled lung and heart; cubes of pig chaps and spine; and tender head pieces and teeth extracted during ceremonial family battles for contents of pig's maw. Such occasions are also known to stir poetic feelings stored always in every romantic Magyar like fat cells:

> When this pig lived
> it would lie and wallow.
> Now its tail
> easy to swallow.

Leaving behind the bones to soak for later, we find that conversations, or "chewing fat," is best way to acquire more urban taste for a country. Magyars will disgorge well-placed words for visitors during short, mid-morning digestion intervals and in afternoon dialysis sessions.

This discovery of talk as a possible sometime oral activity is laid of course to the feet of Sigmund Kopecky, the Wizard of Kapuvar and Father of Psychiatry.

He is that same Sigmund Kopecky who was once an enemy of the state. First came his early idealistic attempts to prevent profaning of the canned fish industry as a member of the Hungarian Cod Squad. Then he slipped into counter-revolutionary schemes, forming Hungarian Bull Mousse Party and uncorking infamous Hungarian Wine Revolt by making advantages of growing popular sediment with a subversive anthem, "Take Me to Your Liter."

Since the counterrevolution was suitably minced, the authorities determined that Kopecky had been after all diseased. He was, thanks to the state, cured—in a smokehouse with pepper and damp.

Kopecky of course turned to psychiatry, and great wisdom flowed always from his simple question and answering sessions with ordinary Magyars on meaty subjects:

> Q. What does Hungarian look for in a wife?
> A. Marbling.
> Q. What is cause of husband-wife disintegrations?
> A. Marriage has not been consommé.
> Q. Why so bitter are Hungarian divorce cases?
> A. At stake is custard of children

Such conversation dainties merely confirmed the theories of Kopecky that all mental disease is ptomanic-depressive and stemming from rotten fish.

Kopecky heroically interrupted snacks to show that one side of a man's head is stimulated by terrifying hungers, but other is willing to wait for seasonings with relish. One part wants to eat the moon; other is content with take-out orders. It is this power of self-transcending that is the key to man's salivation.

As no surprise to anyone, Kopecky's corpse is now in a glass dessert case tastefully embalmed in the Canned Cod Hall of Fame. A plaque of commemoration boils down to a tasty lump his life's work. "Here," the plaque reads, "is a man who settled on fish when chips were down."

But we cannot, as we would like, tarry at this immortal shrine overlong. Visit to Hungary would be hardly complete without the satisfaction of sinking the teeth into additional local culture, such as the Croat International Festival of Horse Chowder to celebrate the canning of horse tongue and burning of books.

To open the festival, the succulent Zoltan Kopecky this year devours Hungarian horse-based dainties, and minor functionaries in supplementary Fishtival lubricate the crowds with beads of ripened carp roe.

Season-defying peasants queue up for viewing the Mlasavec Kopecky "Believe It or Not" collection of edible filth, and seasoned, defiled lady pyrogranite workers from the Zsolnay works at Pecs demonstrate staggered chewing exercises for reducing to recyclable creamy pulp corrugation and also good for making presentable ersatz encrusted yams.

For the highlight of the Fishtival, Ferenc Kopecky demonstrates that the revelations of the Hungarian "Food-a-Rama" of 1294 A.D. had been stolen by the so-called "Italian Renaissance." The Italians were late in learning that actually a new time of respect was merited by the superior shelf life of mankind. This discovery, along with greatest era in world art, was disgorged by Hungarian geniuses who worked ravenously on beautiful landscapes until land was stripped, and it was found that paint is also palatable. In winning his case, Kopecky discloses that Italians cause indigestion, they wear white sheets, and they speak foreign gibberish.

On last night in Szekszard is perhaps some time to sandwich in trip to nightclub, maybe to hear a celebrity like the chewy Ludovic Kopecky who can at same time engulf large fritters and baste out a popular song with a rousing popover:

> Heigh-ho, heigh-ho.
> Magyars are too sweet to spit.
> Unless Bulgarians absorb
> the bulk of it.
> But for finest sweets in bulk, fit
> to overcome rigors of nonbeing
> and rainy season in Pest, the best
> is aromatized, easily metabolized
> Szolucukor pellet (taste swell)—it
> reduce feeling of impotence;
> price, too, makes sense.
> Thanks to Thee, Hungary:
> for glucose in the veins
> during greasy winter rains,
> for anise and for peppermint,
> and less-than-most tooth stains.
> O thanks for the succor
> of Szolucukor.

In hearing this song there is something touched in all of us. We are absorbed in Magyar sentiment—we *are* Hungary! So we will throw of course ourselves at the feet of world markets after sound packaging decisions. And we think as we say good-bye to exercise at the proper moment sanitary controls. But we have learned that also our lives must be always nibbled and savored for surely we will all dissolve soon in the last long dusk like ox-blood bouillon cubes.

10.

Creating Bunched Binds III

This third example of bunched binding may not appear to be a self-evident case of parodic bunching—until the end of the piece. But then, as I note in my blueprint, the parody is revealed as an extreme conceit, a hoaxy effort to jam together written and visual material (the high-tone litcrit term for which is *ut pictura poesis*).

That isn't the only hoax. For instance, there is no such thing, in my view, as "*Yin-Yang* Satire," a subtype that is proposed in the parody. Instead, there are standard-issue multistable applications of the parodic technique that permeate satire as well as other genres, and this multistability is typically generated by presenting parodic terms of contrast as ambiguously linked alternatives. The result of such multistable pairings is, I believe, equivalent to *Yin-Yang* dualism, with its reciprocal and complementary terms of contrast. But all of this is a component of satire only when it is visited by parody.

Another hoaxy element: I'm not quite the racist or sexist that my parody's implied author seems to be. I moved a bit in this ugly direction to make a point, one that's also mentioned in the blueprint: too much of what purports to be satire in this era is pretty gentle stuff, whereas the generic soul of satire is partially lodged in the somewhat neglected Swiftian wing of the form. Such stuff is not only raw and rough but also a reflection of human rage in its most irrational and uncontrolled written frothings. My contention is, without the vital technical bedmate of parody, satire, as a genre, would amount at best to little more than various degrees of splenetic ranting.

Parody Work Sheet

TITLE

> "The Portrait of Satire"

VARIATIONS

Bangs:	Binds:	Blends:
Yes ~~No~~	Yes ~~No~~	Yes ~~No~~
Major ~~Minor~~	Major ~~Minor~~	Major ~~Minor~~

ITERATIVE DETAILS

STYLISTIC / NARRATIONAL CONTRASTS

> A general parody spoof that flows back and forth between
> a mock scholarly style and intrusive, slangy familiarity. Some
> specific parody (in the case of Barthell Cooter).

FORMAL / STRUCTURAL CONTRASTS

> An extreme instance of bunched binding: prose
> pseudo-scholarship morphs into a piece of visual art.

OTHER CONTRASTS

> Plenty of banging puns and one-liners.

COMMENTS

> Bigotry is among the last taboos remaining in our time. I added
> trace elements of it ("Carve Diem" and the mildly racist
> Portrait) to generate multistable doubts about my motives and to
> reflect the fact that satire is often nasty stuff.

THE PORTRAIT OF SATIRE

It's high time that you Culture Vultures out there see some X-ray pics of the inner workings of satire, because your sleek, satiric masterpieces with their succulent but confusing mixtures of piety and rage secretly sustain all plant and animal life on this planet.

First of all, if the satirist's anger is under control, and there is a gassy moral air about the writing, along with a lot of egghead ideas and cheap little bleeding-heart social blueprints, then the work is either a poorly edited Pizza Hut menu or a Utopian Satire:

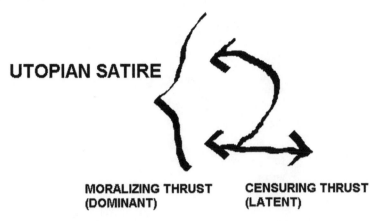

UTOPIAN SATIRE

MORALIZING THRUST (DOMINANT)

CENSURING THRUST (LATENT)

Conversely, if the satirist has the good sense to dampen his moral posturing and to unleash his hatred on the entire world (or at least on the population of Canada), then he has probably written a standard-fare Demonic Satire:

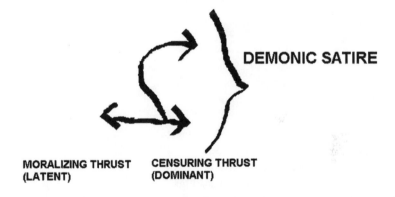

DEMONIC SATIRE

MORALIZING THRUST (LATENT)

CENSURING THRUST (DOMINANT)

Now for some explanatory examples. One of the most endearing Utopian Satires is Laurence Ventricle's poem "Kahlil Gibran, A Short Prophecy":

> An old man
> asked for cider
> and went from house to house
> until he got some free.
> "You are a mystic," we said.
> "There are three
> ways to spot a mystic:

he must be old,
have few desires,
but be obsessed
with seeking what the rest of us
deride as being whimsical
until
it bursts upon our epoch."
"Live intensely,"
the old man mused.
We were still.
He rose
to toss away his cider
and to mutilate
his nose.

Ventricle's poem is a standard Utopian performance, "heavy" message and all. It reveals that the old man, like all wonderful "prophets without honor," has had the moral strength to become a "nosy out-cider."

On the other hand, a typical Demonic Satire, such as Vincent Peel's poem, "*Carve Diem*," is less theoretical and more mutilitarian:

Who here hasn't heard
of the irate invader,
of the grieving good Morrie
who went for Ms. Waters,
who tasted the tale
of that tart-turned-betrayer,
and then in an art shop
became a tattooer,
rose up to resistance
and redeemed his rage.
Now the pales and the pinks
of his lover's fine features,
the palms and the paps
have been purpled with prose.

Who here hasn't heard
of the wit-ridden-writer,
of the cool clever Morrie
who carved out a moral,
who wailed that his name
was just writ in Waters,

but then in that art shop,
bold as a bardic scop,
fought with his furies
and thus seized *the* phrase:
now the word is made flesh
in the curves of his cutie,
the muscles and mounds
read, "Momento Morrie."

Peel's poem, of course, is a satire on the power of positive inking.

Surprise, surprise! Conflicting impulses are at work in satire. It's as if rabies had been combined with lockjaw. As a result of its hellish mixtures, most familiar forms of satire are, in the end, deliciously irresolvable or hilariously anticlimactic. The work may undergo a narrative buildup that rumbles fearfully into existence like a volcano, but the satire will usually sputter out like a seismic poo-poo cushion.

Consider, for instance, the fate of Astrophel Sloat in Loomis Tumid's Utopian novel, *The Social Contract, or, Veneer Disease.*

Our heroine searches selfishly for happiness until she finds that the good people at Schneider's Furniture City have sacrificed their own financial well-being in order to offer her (and feckless mankind) co-polymer, high-density, Turkish Provincial bedroom suites preceded by astonishing dinette overtures in A-flat.

At Schneider's Astrophel learns the philosophy of the "gang" in sales along with the wisdom of shrewd little Moe and the other impish "skip-tracers" in the credit department. Inspired by Moe's teachings, Astrophel joins a group of Neo-Thomist asphalt salesmen and plans a masterwork, *An Ontological Roof for the Existence of God.*

Unfortunately, the ills of the "real world" take their toll, and Astrophel abandons her roofers after she has contracted shingles. In a manner that resembles other Demonic and Utopian Satires, there is a final jarring collapse, and the forces of darkness zap the forces of light. By novel's end, Astrophel, the girl who had sought to become a lamp of truth, has degenerated into a mere dim fixture in the shingles bar scene.

Fortunately, there is an antidote to all of this, a kind of satire with a flavor that does not fade like its self-deflating relations. In this fancy kind of satire, the lockjaw has been partially lifted, and the rabies has been rendered into a foamy kind of love.

The result is a mysteriously ironic kind of cosmic soap opera that leaves you as uneasy as that notorious cocktail, The Bull and Bear, which, apart from the 190-proof vodka, consists of equal portions of Kaopectate and Haley's M-O.

In this, your high-status satire, opposing currents seem to alternate as smoothly as Chiclets in the mouth-to-mouth gum-swapping ceremonies that seal Oriental wedding vows. And because the antagonistic elements appear to coexist in harmony, such satire is like the Oriental idea of *Yin* and *Yang* (a basis for conceptual thinking as important to your Orientals as Platonism in ancient Greece or cowpies in modern Kansas).

Actually, the satirist who adapts a *Yin-Yang* approach tries to breed as much confusion as cosmic harmony because, if nobody figures out what the damn thing really means, then the satirist will be revered as a profoundly multifaceted explorer of life's mysteries—like Deaf Smith or "The Waltz King of Cracow."

In short, when imponderable irony grapples with impenetrable murk, the result is either a gala evening with the Antichrist or

YIN-YANG SATIRE

MURKY DUALITY

MORALIZING THRUST CENSURING THRUST

AC - DC

Here it would be possible to cite numerous illustrative examples, but there is no better example of *Yin-Yang* Satire than Barthell Cooter's brilliant novella, *Better Example*, which, by the gracious permission of Cooter's plumber, is unclogged here in its entirety:

> *Orifice awakened. He was miles long. Why am I named Orifice, he asked.*
> *I will pave the entire North American continent, he answered. Every inch. From sea-to-sea, one continent, under pavement, with tailpipes to fondle for all.*
> *In the next indentation, Baron Yeast awakened also. He awoke because he was no longer sleeping. His sleep had been miles long.*
> *They can paint this continental highway, this U.S. Sea-to-Sea, any color they want, the Baron said. As long as they paint it red.*
> *finis*

Now what can your ordinary digitalis-popping reader make of this thing? Is it, for instance, a symbolic version of the Orpheus-Euridice myth (Orifice-U.S. Sea-to-Sea), or is Orifice merely a car-crazy pervert who can be expected simply to grope tailpipes until he falls, exhausted? Also, what is this "miles long" business (and why is he undercapitalized)? Furthermore, who is Baron Yeast? Is he merely a late riser, or does Baron Yeast represent our Risen Lord? Finally, where is all this leading? The highway will be painted red—why red?

The story, in other words, might be on the straight-and-narrow, or it could be a neo-Commie plot.

Yin-Yang Satire, in short, facilitates all manner of analytic gabble about Romantic Irony, iron-on decals, and what goes good with okra. And with the inclusion of this unfamiliar *Yin-Yang* subgenre, the missing links are in place, and *all* the ingredients of satire are at hand.

It remains only to complete the Portrait because, even though the basic goodies have been sketched, a clear picture of satire does not emerge until the various parts have been assembled:

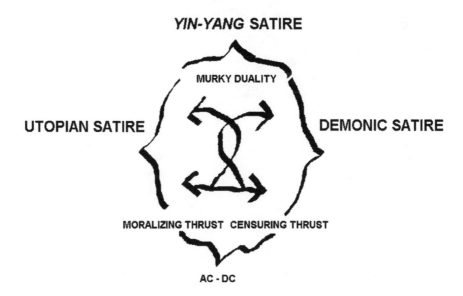

And now for the *pièce de résistance*. When we strip away the useless words surrounding our wholly revealing skeletal view, we find that satire is dominated by the Oriental cast of its greatest examples.

We have before us a Portrait with a universally mysterious resonance, a male Mona Lisa from Old Chinatown. That face is as vaguely unsettling as Warner Oland's passive blend of humility and hauteur in *Charlie Chan Chows Down*.

Here is a mask that is neither comic nor tragic—the Inscrutable Portrait of Satire.

11.

Creating Blended Mimicry I

In the next three chapters, I will be discussing parodic blends in terms of specific parodies that mimic individuals, and then I will devote three chapters to those blended mutations I call "general parody spoofs." These, to refresh your memory, like other blended mutations, create contrasts primarily with their own innards instead of with external models. My examples, then, will be drawn from the two little genres that are the most accessible kinds of writing in each major iterative wing of parodic blending:

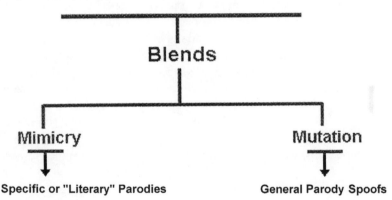

Mimicry, I think, is simply a talent, and that means you've either got more-than-average ability or you don't. But I've always thought everyone has some hardwired ability to mimic others. It's probably a Darwinian coping mechanism that chimps and dolphins, among other life forms, have also seemingly acquired. But the distance between day-to-day mimicry and truly professional-level stuff is vast, and the latter can't really be taught.

Even garden-variety mimicry is a formidable creation, although most of us take it wholly for granted. With mimicry, Party A is simultaneously imitating and not imitating Party B: two voices are being presented at once, and sorting them out or discerning where one begins and the other ends is exceedingly elusive and, if you will, multistable.

I'm not much of a mimic, either vocally, as an occasional amateur thespian, or in writing, as a sometime parodist. So I suggest that those with my limited ability may want to get their feet wet by attempting some Plan B parodic variations on pre-existing parodic works, the choices based on writing that's loaded with one or more accessible sets of odd, mimicry-ready conventional features. Your result—a parody of a parody—may sound as multitiered and confusing as a Wall Street derivative, but Plan B hommage is relatively easy to fabricate as well as clean, legal, and unlikely to cost the nation trillions.

Alternatively, you can decide bravely to go direct and create your mimicry from scratch. In that case, you should choose to mimic subjects who have blazingly distinctive mannerisms and/or those who are language-challenged or language-raping unintentional self-parodists. That is what I have done in this and the two following chapters: I've found material that almost begs either to be parodized or to be reworked in new parodic directions.

The victim, er, subject in my first example of specific parody is stand-up comedian Jeff Foxworthy. He has long been a successful comic, but he became a major phenomenon both in stand-up and in publishing when he devised his one-liner formula for bangingly identifying American rednecks and assorted trailer trash. The format includes such samples as this: "You might be a redneck if…you go to family reunions to meet women." In recent years, Foxworthy has continued to flourish, but he has tended to downplay his famous formula, presumably for the understandable reason of not wanting to be forever labeled One-Note Jeff. That's too bad because, while some of his books, calendars, and rent-a-redneck franchises included some clunkers, much of what he has produced in this arena is exceedingly witty.

That one-note concern should not deter you, a budding parodist, from adopting and adapting Foxworthy's groundbreaking anthropological scholarship for your own parodic devices. In the example below, I've reworked Foxworthy's parodic format to assault Middle Americans, many of whom constitute a distinct semi-redneck breed in their own right. But you can come up with a grab bag of variations all your own. Examples: "You might be a Croatian if…," or "You might be from Brooklyn if…," or something gloriously bizarre such as "You might be turning into a Shih-Tzu if…"

Parody Work Sheet

TITLE

> "You Might Be a Mid-Wreck If ..."

VARIATIONS

Bangs:	Binds:	Blends:
Yes ~~No~~	Yes ~~No~~	Yes ~~No~~
Major ~~Minor~~	Major ~~Minor~~	Major ~~Minor~~

ITERATIVE DETAILS

STYLISTIC / NARRATIONAL CONTRASTS

> For the most part, this is a spoof essay about rednecks and Midwesterners. A relatively straightforward style sets up an array of gags, including puns.

FORMAL / STRUCTURAL CONTRASTS

> The essay is a little less than 1,150 words and consists mostly of parodic bangs, but the closing bow to Jeff Foxworthy (a little less than 350 words) dominates the essay.

OTHER CONTRASTS

> Foxworthy's setup/hook ("You might be a redneck if ...") has been adapted/stolen, and the borrowed hook ("YOU MIGHT BE A MID-WRECK IF") appears just once but sets up 21 one-liners.

COMMENTS

> A case can be made that this essay represents, at best, extreme homage and, at worst, theft. But I prefer to envision it as mimicry that has the effect of binding rednecks to new kin.

YOU MIGHT BE A MID-WRECK IF...

The Old South is now largely populated by refugees who have fled there from Ottumwa, Iowa, and other Midwestern cities, all of which are imploding because of that region's well-known problems—horrific cold spells, industrial decline, and pan-national Rotarian fundamentalism.

Sadly, despite the weight of numbers, a transplanted Midwesterner will not be accepted readily in the South unless he happens to be a rock star in a stock car.

More likely, that melodious Magnolia Princess who charms a Midwestern newcomer with "hey-hi-yew" expressions of interest and concern will refer to him behind his back as "a two-hundred-pound Polish sausage."

In other words, those who expect to transplant the seemingly straightforward and rational communications strategies of the Rustbelt ("Ottumwa, let us reason together...") will discover that Reason is as inappropriate in the South as is a nose job on an anteater.

In desperation, some Midwesterners attempt to "fit in" by way of camouflage. Bookstores are filled with volumes purporting to tell an outsider how to think and talk like a Southerner as well as how to cook such redneck favorites as "White Bread and Catsup Surprise," "Rooster Tartare," and "Tomcat Espadrille."

A Midwestern chef once tried to assimilate by introducing his own version of redneck cuisine. He clicked at first, devising some interesting regional dishes with Quikrete cement and Atomic Fire Balls.

But he bombed when he tried to pass off live termite swarms as "redneck sushi." His rationale was, since Japanese sushi chefs can make a selling point out of not cooking the food, their redneck counterparts ought to be able to up the ante and claim that food is better if you don't kill it.

Now that chef is back in Milwaukee where he belongs. Today he has a successful, nonethnic restaurant, The Eating Disorder, famous for its angel-hair dish made with pine nuts and low-test nylon fishing line.

Let's face it, that chef and other Ottumwans could never have passed for Southerners. That virtually ineradicable Midwestern accent is a dead giveaway. Your basic Midwest redneck equivalent uses his nasal passages, rather than his mouth, for oral communication (and for God knows what else). Even those Midwesterners who do utilize their lips and jaws properly do so with a grating whine, as if their nostrils were being extruded through their teeth.

In my view, social integration down South can only come to those Midwesterners able to get in touch with their own core culture. This is what I mean: our country's weird, terrifying center is the natural habitat of smiling, soft-spoken serial killers.

The Midwest has the broadest variety of ethnic and racial diversity, but a rigid basis for cultural cohesion was supplied long ago by the region's pioneering Germanic settlers. Your basic Midwesterner combines a crude and pathological materialism, a polka-laced oompah-pah extroverted heartiness, and an apparent open-book personality that actually masks deep repression and a twisted inner life.

Expect to find in the typical Middie a psychotic reverence for cleanliness, authority, and order; a love of Nuremberg-style football stadium rallies; and the secret belief that, had things worked out a little differently, Jeffrey Dahmer might have made one hell of an effective American politician.

Midwestern *volk*, in other words, are America's Nazis. So there's hope for their assimilation down South, because Southerners readily relate to fascism and because in the South violence solves everything. Remember that loveable Midwesterner Ed Gein? A few decades ago he murdered his neighbors and turned their skin into lampshades? There's a little bit of Ed in all Middies.

There must be something about the sun in the middling latitudes that has affected this breed as surely as cosmic rays reddened poor tenant farmers' necks in the South. That's why my own private generic tag for those from the Central States is "mid-wrecks"—their twisted, kitschy, often-psychotic values have been baked into their geins.

As far as melting into the Southern pot is concerned, my advice to the mid-wreck is to flaunt rather than to downplay your origins. The South is not zoned off just by the Mason-Dixon Line. It's a state of mind bounded by Virginia and schizophrenia, by Texas and excess. If you're crazy enough, you'll eventually fit in down there.

So how do you tell if you're the right kind of mid-wreck, a candidate for a permanent Dixie Green Card?

With a salute to the methodology of the great Jeff Foxworthy (creator of the "You Might Be a Redneck If..." empire), I want to present some guidelines for determining whether you're the real Midwest McCoy (or Hatfield).

Let this short catalog be your compass:

You might be a mid-wreck if...

- Your surname has at least ten letters, only two of which are vowels.

- Your favorite *aprés*-sex activity is a bristle-brush scrub down with Comet.

- You hate antiques because they are "old and dirty," but you *do* horde "comfortable collectibles," such as shiny, new Barcaloungers, preferably those with tail fins.

- Your secret ambition is to own an FM radio station with an all-accordion format.

- Your hobby is covering bowling balls with *macramé*.

- You're sexually aroused by the Pillsbury Bake-Off.

- You're a status-seeker driven "to keep up with the Cvetanovskis."

- You'd love to serve the homeless, but you can't find a large enough Jell-O mold to put them in.

- Childhood games with your dolls, Barbie and Ken, featured lots of bondage and degradation.

- You need to join a twelve-step "recovery program," but you won't commit to it because the membership hasn't been unionized.

- Your favored sexual positions are at your mate's feet or throat.

- Your wine cellar is organized according to the year of the pressing, but the selection is exclusively Cold Duck.

- You paint cheery greetings and family surnames (such as "Hi, We're the Keisters") on your mobile home, on your Lava Lite, and on the corpses you're collecting in the crawl space.

- You can't resist "hitting on" old people and children, especially when your lampshades need to be re-covered.

- You've done unspeakable things with Italian sausages, but the *wurst* is yet to come.

- Your motorhome includes a shrine to Lawrence Welk.

- You're a charter member of Women's Liberace.

- You met your wife when you were both selected as Greater Milwaukee Troll Doll Look-Alikes.

- You plan to join The Hair Club for Men/Women, but you're considering taxidermy as an alternative.

- You write love poems to walleyed pikes.

- You like to keep plenty of Blue Nuns in the fridge to serve company, but the larger ones will only fit in the freezer.

This list of symptoms could be expanded indefinitely, but you now have food for thought. Be sure to surround it with such favored mid-wreck "accompaniments" as cheese food, Cool Whip, or Tang.

Sieg hi-y'all.

12.

Creating Blended Mimicry II

As a mimic with minimal aptitude, I have angled my instruction to continue traipsing down the path of least resistance: specifically parodizing Richard M. Nixon and similar odd ducks should be as easy for you as it is for me. People who are clearly miserable inhabiting their own skins, like our thirty-seventh president, tend to rely on a repetitive package of stock phrases to get them through their days and nights, and if their vocation is politics or sales or any other people-beseeching enterprise, those stock phrases usually reek of insincerity and fake glad-handing drenched in a poisonous perfume of clichés. All you need to do is to pepper a parody with generous sprinklings of your target's slimy stock phrases, apparent in any number of transcripts or film clips, and you've *got* your man (or woman).

And, with Nixon, you get a corrupt, venomous politician seething with paranoia and rage, a package that seeped into his public persona and that controlled the private man, as miles of audio tape have revealed. For the smarmy flavor of Nixon's public rhetoric and the rhythms of his speech, I particularly recommend a visit to the Internet transcript of the September 23, 1952, "Checkers Speech," in which he, desperate to remain Eisenhower's VP candidate, defended the exposure of a secret fund established by his supporters during his then-ongoing term in the U. S. Senate. At the end of his speech, Nixon confided this immortal nugget to the national TV audience: "One other thing I probably should tell you because if we don't they'll probably be saying this about me too, we did get something—a gift—after the election. ...You know what it was. It was a little cocker spaniel dog in a crate....And our little girl—Tricia, the 6-year old—named it Checkers. And you know, the kids, like all kids, love the dog and I just want to say this right now, that regardless of what they say about it, we're gonna keep it."

If someone like Nixon seems too dated for you to mimic in five-finger parodic exercises, then I suggest you tackle a comic icon of more recent vintage like George W. Bush. Despite being a narcissistic frat-boy prince, he fits the Nixonian mold because of an apparently severe case of dyslexia that made his public pronouncements a twisted, phony mess, an endless stream of "Bushisms." I refer you to such Bush-botched Internet collections as this one: http://politicalhumor. about.com/library/blbushisms.htm.

For what it's worth, I am an equal opportunity despiser of all politicians and all political parties (other than the Guelphs), but, for some reason, I find right-leaning politicians easier to parodize than those on the left. Perhaps, it's because the former sometimes claim that they uphold high standards of decency and morality, the often-sham nature of which is pleasurable to expose. "There's no bottom to the Left," maintains a Rutgers University professor I met some months ago, and maybe that's why I'm not drawn to mimic those of that ilk—if there's no there there, as Gertrude Stein famously said about Oakland, California, where's the fun or the comic hook?

Back to Nixon. I remember an old joke, the seven-word punch line of which seems to sum up the out-of-synch discomfort of the man. *Set-up:* What is a Richard Nixon skin-diving outfit? *Punch line:* a blue, three-piece, pin-striped suit.

In my blueprint below, I mention having read "The Dark Comedian," an essay about Nixon in a 1988 issue of *Time* magazine. Not only did the essay confirm my lifelong feeling that Nixon, in all his ugly squalor, was unintentionally hilarious, but it also inspired me to imagine that a perpetually shameless Nixon might actually read *Time* and then try to determine if a few post-Watergate bucks could be made from a stand-up routine.

In short, while my little specific parody attempts to mimic Nixon, it also bunch binds the thirty-seventh president to a one-liner stand-up comedy routine:

Parody Work Sheet

TITLE

> "Richard Nixon's Last Stand-Up"

VARIATIONS

Bangs:	Binds:	Blends:
Yes ~~No~~	Yes ~~No~~	Yes ~~No~~
Major ~~Minor~~	Major ~~Minor~~	Major ~~Minor~~

ITERATIVE DETAILS

STYLISTIC / NARRATIONAL CONTRASTS

> In part a specific parody that attempts to capture Nixon's phony bonhomie and false moralizing, his aggression, paranoia, and self-justification.

FORMAL / STRUCTURAL CONTRASTS

> The aim here is parodic binding, but it is arguable that Nixon the ex-prez and Nixon the terrible comedian are all of a piece. However, with the real Nixon the comedy was unintentional.

OTHER CONTRASTS

> An occasion for parodic bangs in the form of a bad generic stand-up comedy routine.

COMMENTS

> *Man of the Year* (2006) with Robin Williams is about a comedian-president. A funny Nixon was anatomized by Roger Rosenblatt's "The Dark Comedian," *Time*, April 25, 1988.

RICHARD NIXON'S LAST STAND-UP

He's long dead now, so let the historians sort out what's important. Sure, he had a stand-up routine. But he only did one performance. Why did he bother? Well, he missed the arena, and an essay in Time *magazine called him the great "Dark Comedian" of the age. So, what the hell, he decided to give it a shot. How do I know all this? I was granted "special access" before and after the show because we both kept up with the baseball and because, hey, I kissed some ass. Yes, the press had been notified, but just one of the print boys showed. He was a liberal, naturally, a reviewer from* The Newark Star-Ledger. *His was the sole record of that June night in 1990 at the Komedy Klub, but only a little summary crumb from his story appeared in the paper. You want some irony: the story was cut to shreds, the editors claimed, because of "family values issues." I suspect the story mostly disappeared because, for once, Mr. Nixon had been quoted accurately. Because I care, I managed to get ahold of the reporter's hard copy, the computer printout of his whole story. Here's how the evening was originally reported:*

Richard Nixon lurched out, living and dead, into the painful spotlight like some George Romero ghoul. Sweating, squinting, his eyes as impenetrable as Bakelite, he launched right into his *shtick*.

"Good evening, my fellow Americans.

"You know, it hasn't been easy, my life.

"Even my marriage—Pat and I have had to work hard at our marriage. I just happen to love those corny old 'Ma and Pa Kettle' movies with Marjorie Main and Percy Kilbride, and, you know, Pat just can't stand them.

"Well, Pat's got a doozy of a bad habit herself. She started smoking marijuana after I left the White House. "Well, I just don't approve...because it's *wrong*. You know what Pat tells me? She says, 'Dick, this is just another case of the kettle calling the pot black.'

"Actually, Pat got very depressed when the crooks forced me out of the White House. But neither one of us are quitters. That's not in our vocabulary.

"I'll bet you didn't know that Pat was so depressed by the dirty tricks our enemies played on us that she walked out on me for a while. She took up with one of those Jap vibrators, and let me make this perfectly clear: Pat said the vibrator was a better listener than me.

"And the vibrator had grown, and I hadn't.

"Well, I don't like to mess with sex, and I certainly don't believe in extramarital kissy-face. But Dick Nixon can only take so much.

"So for a while I had a little, you know, an intimate *tête-à-tête* going with one of those bank all-time teller machines. That lasted until the machine found out I was making deposits all over town.

"The machines shut me down, so I worked at not thinking about sex for a while. And I tried to lift my spirits by reading inspirational books.

"There's just so many of these to choose from in this great country of ours. I like *The Joy of Grunting, See You at the Bottom,* and *Think and Grow Numb.* "But I couldn't keep my mind off 'the dating scene.'

"It's too bad that women these days don't appreciate my old-fashioned romantic gestures. I try to whisper into a woman's ear sweet nothings about oral history and oral sex. Then I like to show her my stretch marks.

"Part of my problem was, I chose women who weren't available. Probably, I should've stopped hanging around funeral homes.

"And I wasn't relaxed about sex because I don't ever want anybody seeing me naked. That's why with Pat I always chose to be on the bottom—underneath the mattress.

"Another thing—having so many enemies attack me without provocation during my life has made me suspicious. But even when I had a tough time with dating, I still liked to hope there was a special someone out there, someone I could hold in my arms, secure in the knowledge that she was poisoning my tropical fish.

"So I tried to find a nice woman. I knew that we'd probably be too suspicious to have sex at first, but I thought that maybe we could waylay each other. But I was wrong. Only Pat and I could do that.

"So Pat and I got back together. Pat and I resumed our marriage, and for a while our sex life was what you hep cats would call 'hotsy-totsy.' I'll confess that we even got involved with kinky equipment and weird sexual paraphernalia. But, you know, our love life was never the same after the dialysis machine broke down."

Nixon was sweating hard, but he was getting some laughs. They weren't what you'd call *comfortable* laughs.

"It was always tough for us," he said. "We had a tough time just having children. Believe me, it was work.

"First of all, Pat wanted to remain a virgin, even after we married. She said that she was saving herself for divorce.

"Well, we couldn't have a child under those circumstances, so we did the next best thing. We bought a trash compactor. And I'm proud to say that I personally handled the midnight feedings.

"But we still hadn't created our family, our wonderful children, Tricia and Julie, and our little dog, Checkers. So Pat and I went to the doctor to see if there was something physically wrong with us.

"And, you know, that led to another crisis because it turned out that my sperm was regular, but Pat could only take premium or unleaded.

"The doctor said that we had two choices. We could go to a sperm bank, or we could go to an adoption agency. Pat decided on the sperm bank because my wife, Pat, has always been a frugal Republican lady.

"And, you see, when you open an account at the sperm bank, they give you a toaster.

"I want you to know that going to a sperm bank forces you to make very complicated and emotional choices. We looked at a lot of sperm, and we finally narrowed the decision down to three candidates—imitation orange, raspberry, and lime."

After a long riff about working in a dildo factory, the ex-president, to use his final words from the stage, "petered out." The lights went down, and there was a little scattered applause.

Later, drenched in flop sweat and his own peculiar hormonal gumbo, Nixon received his family and friends, who included a crowd from the State Department and the U.N. And he answered their inevitable questions.

No, he wouldn't settle for the second spot on anybody's ticket, and no, he wouldn't sign on as a lounge act in Vegas or anywhere else.

Nixon was restless. His behavior seemed manic, particularly when he demanded that everyone "stow the chit-chat and talk turkey." Then he flapped his arms, making strange gobbler noises.

Nixon was queried about the difficult U.S. relations with China. "I don't have any Chinese relations," he said. "But you don't know *difficult* until you've had an Irish mother-in-law.

"She told me that her daughter's marriage had been made in heaven, and then she burned a cross in our front yard.

"That lady said to me, 'Dick Nixon, you're a real sickola.' That was her attitude, but let me make this perfectly clear: it didn't stop her from borrowing my pantyhose."

Asked to comment on the economic policies of his successors, Nixon produced a large aluminum coin and proposed that it be issued to commemorate their various programs. The group played along and protested jovially that both sides of the coin were blank.

"That's it," Nixon said. "You can't make heads or tails of these guys."

Then he invited a well-wisher's teenage boy to come forward. He indicated that the kid was part of a charade that also included the ex-president turning his back and dropping his pants.

What did it all mean?

"Moon Young Son," Nixon beamed.

Just as his behavior appeared to be verging on the monumentally bizarre, Nixon assumed the mantle of world leader, explaining with the gravest dignity the real point of his little charade.

"I wanted you all to get a handle on the 'Nude Nixon,'" he said.

"That's a little shameless, isn't it," someone giggled.

"Shamelessness is easy; comedy is hard," intoned the thirty-seventh president of the United States, who then, with a hitherto unnoticed pig's bladder, gaveled the session to a close.

13.

Creating Blended Mimicry III

The diction and speech rhythms of a slightly lost and out-of-it cub scout in the service of a camping, highly passive-aggressive, but occasionally caterwauling male who was one of history's great voyeurs and gossips and who also happened to have unlimited access to *people-who-matter*, if only for a short mattering span, and to a sad, endless crew of people who wanted to matter—at almost any cost—but didn't. That's the essence of *The Andy Warhol Diaries*, my third exemplary starting point for those would-be specific parodists who are like me in not being natural mimics.

Once again: I urge you to find someone like Warhol, whose stylistic fetishes and sundry obsessions verge on self-parody. Then (a) give your targeted parodee a little prose push of your own devising to send him or her way over the top and (b), to package the material with an extra flourish, encase the parodee in bunched binding. In other words locate your target in a strange profession or setting or lifestyle. Immerse your target in odd combinations that are as inappropriate as possible. Thus, just as my parodic Nixon was a nightclub comic, my parodic version of Andy Warhol has been lashed to Alan Greenspan, then-chairman of the Federal Reserve.

My parody, while attempting to mimic Warhol, does so under the pretense that the now-slightly-disgraced former Fed Chairman had not only ghostwritten the Warhol *Diaries* but also that this furtive handiwork had been unwittingly revealed by the publication of Greenspan's own diaries, which mirror the style and sensibility of the earlier volume. In this way, my specific parody attempts to mimic an Andy Warhol who has been bound and bunched into the world of economics and finance.

For capturing the flavor of Warhol, you will find an endless resource in the *Diaries*. With the help of the unfailingly fascinating *Diaries*, your own prose can quickly take on a whimpering, simpering, mincing life of its own (and you'll then be in a position not only to parodize Warhol but also to handle others, such as filmmaker David Lynch, who also depends on kiddie-poo speech patterns in his interviews). To add unmistakable Warhol touches, include lots of parenthetical records of your parodee's incidental expenses and/or parenthetical information about the parodee's caloric intake.

Parody Work Sheet

TITLE

> "Fed Head Co-Pope of Pop"

VARIATIONS

Bangs: Yes ~~No~~ Major ~~Minor~~	Binds: Yes ~~No~~ Major ~~Minor~~	Blends: Yes ~~No~~ Major ~~Minor~~

ITERATIVE DETAILS

STYLISTIC / NARRATIONAL CONTRASTS

> Warhol's prose style invites mimicry: his aggressive faux naïveté gushes with undifferentiated enthusiasm for matters large and small, but there is a sad, jaded omniverousness to it all.

FORMAL / STRUCTURAL CONTRASTS

> There is bunched binding gold in this combination--the semi-orgiastic world of the Factory and Warhol's pop culture omnipresence combined with the hyper-uptight world of the Fed.

OTHER CONTRASTS

> There are few one-liners but plenty of bangs. Many of these arise from the skein of incongruities, but some from the real Warhol's diary record of penny-pinching and calorie counting.

COMMENTS

> The parody, especially its banging, depends to a large degree upon allusion, the effect of which can be sorely dissipated with the passage of time and the descent of allusions into obscurity.

FED HEAD CO-POPE OF POP

The rumor that former Federal Reserve Chairman Alan Greenspan ghostwrote all or part of The Andy Warhol Diaries *careened around the global village last week, gaining velocity as luminaries termed it the most astonishing collaboration between art and commerce since Mogen teamed with David.*

The cause of the commotion was the unauthorized publication last Tuesday of slices from Chairman Greenspan's own diary, the style and content of which so resembles the late Mr. Warhol's that one New York tabloid incautiously headlined, "The Poop—Fed Head Co-Pope of Pop."

As part of his tongue-in-cheek work ethic, Mr. Warhol did recruit pinch-hitters, and he farmed out altogether some of his projects to aspiring clones. So it is conceivable that, as Barron's *put it, "the diary-writing Andy may have appointed his pal Alan 'Chairman of the Hetero-Reserves.'"*

Of more importance, The Alan Greenspan Diaries *uniquely illuminate the mysterious daily inner workings of the Fed. Heretofore, central bankers have been as notoriously secretive as mating muskrats.*

Allegedly, a murky public stance affords the Fed the means to prevent speculators from profitably anticipating changes in monetary policy, grants the Fed room to maneuver freely in times of financial crisis, and allows the Fed to conduct in dignified obscurity during periods of relative calm a top-drawer phone-sex operation.

Now because of the diaries, the veil has been lifted, and the official who was once "the second most powerful man in America" has been revealed as a weird, endearing "party-animal," and not as merely a sinister, one-dimensional, behind-the-scenes manipulator of financial triumphs and disasters like Casey Kasem.

Thanks to these selected excerpts (they are not, as has been reported, "elected sexcerpts"), we now have a definitive portrait: the former chairman, while flaky on the surface, has the homely, all-American staying power of chicken pot pie or a prefrontal lobotomy.

October 6, 1979

It was just too nerve-wracking with Paul Volcker back in town, and both of us knowing that inflation fighting was my genre first, so I, not he, should be the new chairman of the Federal Reserve.

And to think of the times I've taken Jimmy and Roslyn Carter, not to mention that oafish Hamilton Jordan, to Studio 54 with Halston, Liza, Liz, and Ayn Rand. What can they expect from Paul but a few really boring afternoons watching him support the lira?

And now I'm so mad at Diana Vreeland because she's climbed on the Volcker bandwagon. Calvin Klein told her that Paul was going to stop regulating interest rates and let market forces take over. That will push rates up and down like a yo-yo, and Diana said that it would be "so liberating, so like the overthrow of hats and gloves, so like the dear lost excitement of David Bailey's London, and so *chic* in its own sweet, convulsive, 1960s retro manner."

Now, according to Bianca Jagger, Paul is going to ring up John Fairchild and propose for *W* a one-shot revival of Diana's old "People Are Talking About" column to announce the discovery of Paul Volcker and the reemergence of *mauve*.

June 2, 1987

At last, at last, my hour's come round at last! I'm the new chairman (cab fare $3).

I can hardly believe it. But now I have to hurt all the realtors. They're so deliciously tacky, which, of course, is why I've been taking Polaroids and tape recording them for years.

They remind me of Bert Parks, who I've always idolized and who was as mean to me as Truman Capote until Bert decided to "take me up."

And that's what I have to do to short-term interest rates—take them up, up, up. That will butcher the poor realtors, because then they won't be able to sell their cute little houses.

But what can I do? Oberon, my numerologist, wants higher interest rates, so it's out of my control. If I don't give them to her, she'll spend all her time advising people like Bill Blass and Warren Buffett.

All these things are just fated anyway. Like my finding that new magic crystal in that shop on Lexington Avenue.

When the news about my appointment hit, Mick Jagger and Jerry Hall came over with champagne (I took three sips and had two bites from a Mallomar and some crumbs from a dietetic Stella D'Oro).

Jerry seems so bored these days, because Mick isn't really helping her get launched in show business. Since I have to dispose of Townsend-Greenspan to avoid all that stupid conflict-of-interest nonsense, I was hoping that maybe Mick would buy my nice little company for Jerry. It would be a good way for her to learn something about economics.

Then I found out what was really up her sleeve (and it certainly wasn't deodorant). She started lobbying for me to help get her appointed president of the New York Fed because, she said, "trading all that money, bonds, and things would be almost like having orgasms all the time."

Of course, I couldn't go along with that scheme—at least, not right away and not until I give Mike Milken a chance to bid on the whole package. He's got first dibs because I'm just wild about him in his wig and because the boy is going to need to do something after he gets out of the slammer.

October 19, 1987

Sometimes I think the tragedy in my life will never end. John Phelan of the New York Stock Exchange started calling me about 9:00 a.m., just carrying on about how the stupid stock market was going to tank, and then, after it opened, he must have phoned me every fifteen minutes with some new sob story.

How could that man have expected me to sympathize with his little problems when I'm in mourning for my bottle-green piece of Depression glass that Tama Janowitz dropped when her old boyfriend, Ronnie Cutrone, bit her on the leg?

The market was down 508 points when it closed, and Phelan was moaning that he and his little friends and associates were preparing for "the death of the

U.S. equity markets." I had simply had enough and was about to react by saying to all those nosy reporters, "Fine, if the market *soufflé* has collapsed, let them eat *crepes*."

I mean, I was ready to move on to something important, but Ronnie Reagan, of all people, started calling me about this stupid stuff too. So it looks like I'm going to have to slash interest rates (just when they were looking so sinister and so out of control) and make oodles of money available to the brokers and all those other whores.

If I hadn't given Ronnie what he wanted, I simply wouldn't have been able to slip away with Cornelia Guest and go to that party that Matt Dillon and Rob Lowe were tossing in Soho (cab $6).

November 4, 1992

Oh, what a relief! Bye-bye sourpuss Bush and that unspeakable preppie Nick Brady. We had the makings of a really impressive Depression, and they talked me into stopping it and keeping the whole thing really quiet and invisible for four years.

So I quietly slashed rates from 9 percent to 3 percent (I forget all the particulars, and who cares). I dropped bank reserve requirements, defended the damn dollar, and muttered about the national debt. I've done all these other stuffy and "responsible" things, even though a financial panic would have been so much more fun than keeping the banking system alive.

And they never once allowed me to announce on *Larry King Live* that I'd saved the country.

Gosh, it's true: no good deed goes unpunished. How many times did I *not* go shopping so I could lower interest rates for them? And they both kept demanding more. I can only give so much, so Brady just jilted me, cutting *all* social contact. Thank God, Anna Nicole Smith and Kurt Cobain were there to comfort me.

January 3, 1994

Happy New Year to me. The Clintons have done just about everything nice imaginable for this tired old central banker. Like having me sit next to Hillary at the State of the Union speech, and the supremest compliment of all: letting me advise her on makeovers every month.

And the Clintons were responsible for that lovable rapscallion Bob Woodward writing *The Agenda* with the focus on White House economic policy and on me as The Dominant One (hardly my thing...but I'll claim it).

What just makes it perfect is Bob getting it so wrong. Why would I want to see the deficit cut to make all those awful *nouveau riche* bond traders happy? I was merely bemoaning the deficit while toting up my "mad money" account ($34.18) and worrying how the need to impose fiscal discipline was going to upset that wand dealer at the Crystal Dragon in Alexandria.

Talk about current account deficits. That greedy New Ager has been getting rich off poor me. I've bought at least one art nouveau, deco, or moderne wand every single week for the last two months (total: $234.21).

March 5, 1995

If I'm feeling down, shouldn't the economy be depressed too? Okay, so I ratcheted up short-term rates umpteen times in a year, and nothing happened—just a few hedge funds exploded, but no Depression.

The stupid Dow Jones Average rumbled past four thousand even with the peso crisis, the Japanese earthquake, the collapse of Barings, and the breakup of Jerry Seinfeld and Shoshanna Lonstein (thank God, it was only temporary. Sent them some "remaindered" valentine candy: $4.34 + $2.16 postage).

Oh, well. I'll always have plenty of options (so long as I keep delivering inside information to certain trading desks).

Oh, Madonna just sent me a postcard from Miami. She said she'd "meet me at the punchbowl any time" I "want to spike the Fed Funds Rate." Cute.

December 6, 1996

There they go again, as Ronnie Reagan liked to say. (Gosh, I miss the way we used to practice vacant stares on each other).

This time the stock market fell out of bed because everybody thought I was trying to jawbone it down.

Wrong again.

I made a little speech last night and asked, "How do we know when irrational exuberance has unduly escalated asset values?"

Everyone with any sense knows I could care less about stocks, and everyone who cares about me knows that my real worry is something else—all those crazy bidders causing sell-outs and forcing me to rush my cubic zircona and diamonique purchases from QVC and the Home Shopping Network.

April 6, 1997

I just love Bill Clinton. The hair. The glands. I bet he wears gold chains and lots of jewelry under his "uniform," just like me.

I love him for not dumping me for some Democrat when my term was up. But I'd love him anyway. Not just because he can imitate Elvis but because he *is* Elvis.

Speaking of that, I need to remind myself to call him about the two of us maybe printing extra money so we can give pink Cadillacs on the spur of the moment to lots of complete strangers.

Oh, I shouldn't forget to mention that I got married today.

I mean, my dear, I didn't get married, but my new double, Sid Caesar, hitched up (in my name, of course) with some newshound named Andrea Mitchell. My numerologist, Oberon, targeted her because she has the same surname as my first wife, and as Oberon said, "Alphabetic and numeric continuity is just tellingly crucial."

Andrea agreed to be the new Mrs. Greenspan because she wanted the "prestige." God. How boring.

Sid, of course, was willing to become my full-time stand-in for almost no money because he so wants to get back into big-time show business. I'm really excited. Isn't Sid just excruciatingly passé?

I really don't think he looks that much like me—apart from the fact that neither of us has enough hair to manage a really hip comb-over—but no one will even bother to notice that Sid isn't me, anyway.

When I asked Bob Colacello to "pop the question" to Sid, I said, "Tell Mr. Caesar he should want to be my double because we're fellow musicians and maybe even karmic twins" (my God, we both studied the sax at Julliard). But the truth is, Sid was the hire I wanted because he made up all that wonderful foreign double-talk on *Your Show of Shows*.

I want him to spray lots and lots of gobbledy-gook into the speeches he delivers for me and when he's giving my congressional testimony and when he invents new Fed policy for me.

Bob didn't think Sid was a loopy enough stand-in. Bob wanted to find some candidates at the place where he recruited those cross-dressing models for Andy Warhol—The Gilded Grape, which Bob describes as "a bizarre little bar on Eighth Avenue and West Forty-fifth Street." It's supposed to be frequented by black and Hispanic transvestites (average height: six feet two) and white truck-driver types (average weight: 275 pounds).

August 14, 1997
President Bill isn't going to be happy about the crunch I've been launching. But when two friends like Norris Church and Norman Mailer gang up on you, it's hopeless.

Norman says he started off by writing about a great war, and he'd like to top off his career by writing about a great depression. So I've gotten our feet damp by lending a few trillion dollars (really just billions, but "trillions" sounds better) to my favorite currency traders, who are quietly destroying a few stupid Asian economies for me.

But, if having an old-fashioned panic means that Asians are going to start calling me up all the time again, I may not be able to go through with it. They're all in that crazy time zone with the Japanese. Naturally, I'll have to do whatever it takes to stop them from calling me in the middle of *David Letterman*.

Still, I'm excited. Norman says the depression book will be starring *moi*. He's even talking about hiring Paul Morrissey to help make a movie about it that will be four or five *years* long.

December 2, 1997

Wouldn't you know it. The Dow climbed back over eight thousand yesterday, and Sid Caesar, standing in for me as always, gave some kind of "upbeat" speech today. He's also doing something or other with Bob Rubin and Larry Summers to stop my depression, which is now being called "The Asian Contagion." Can't they come up with a sexier name than that?

I'd be a lot madder about this meddling if I hadn't found something major and new to obsess about. I've discovered the World Wrestling Federation and Stone Cold Steve Austin, the Road Dogg, and Bad Ass Billy Gunn.

September 24, 1998

Now Sid has gone and let William McDonough (I think he's with the New York Fed) organize the rescue of Long-Term Capital Management. And they did it just when that one little firm's crash was about to trigger a systemic collapse.

You'd think I'd be furious, but systemic failures are rare and precious, and the hoi polloi shouldn't be allowed to launch one. So I'm thrilled that the Big Bang is still going to be my baby and not the result of some Nobel prize-winning morons being let loose at a hedge fund.

So Sid can do all the propping-up he wants and blather on about good times being justified by technology and the "productivity miracle." Wait till next year. I've got a double-whammy systemic jolt of my own in the works.

And the thing is, I would've probably stepped in to help Long-Term Capital Management anyway. A chunk of the firm belongs (or did belong) to John Meriwether, and he and his friends at Salomon Brothers didn't squeal when they took the heat for my rigging government bond auctions.

March 29, 1999

My extremely small and top-secret Post-Impeachment Victory Party for President Bill is tonight.

Monica Lewinsky will slip in and join him (no pun intended, Dear Diary), and I have O. J. (who's *been there* and who can feel Bill's pain) paired with Denise Rich.

I just had to invite Denise, because I remain Marc's silent partner after all these years and because she's still very close to her ex. I do hope she doesn't sing again tonight—she'll shatter my crystal ball.

And that's the whole guest list.

There's a reason for keeping the group small (and for waiting this long to celebrate). I'm ready to reveal my master plan, and I only want a few trustworthy ears to hear it. I've finally had enough money printed for the mammoth job ahead. I can't wait to put my arm around President Bill, to look into those sleepy Camaro salesman's eyes and tell him we're going to debase the currency together.

For so long now, Norman and Norris have been demanding that I produce "blood in the streets" so he can have a slam-bang ending for his book, *Buggering the Millennium*. And Oberon, too, is long past ready to let the big, bad numerical shoe drop. So it's finally time to let my economic Titanic hit the iceberg…twice.

It's all working out perfectly so far. The Dow actually closed above ten thousand today, and the blind, day-trading fools out there are steering heedlessly and deliciously toward the jaws of that all-devouring Y2K monster. January 1, 2000, won't simply begin an ordinary little depression. It'll be a cataclysm followed by a free fall back to the Stone Age.

The lights and everything else will suddenly go out, and Y2K will shut down the world.

A few weeks into what I'm calling "Crash No. 1" (and shortly after my buddies, two former CIA hotdogs, have terminated Sid Caesar with extreme prejudice), President Bill and I will go before the nation.

He'll say that we're going to stop the bloodshed and panic because we're going to lend every single citizen unlimited amounts of money.

And, boy, for a while I expect there'll be a peppy little recovery. Maybe the lights will even come back on.

By March 2000 or thereabouts, we will have flooded the system with 100 trillion zillion dollars (this time I'm not exaggerating), and, if my calculations are correct, by sometime in April, a two-ounce package of Doritos will cost about 1.35 billion dollars.

By the early fall, we'll be deep into the worst hyperinflation in human history, and the dollar will be totally dead. That'll push us back to a barter economy and lots of looting and shooting again.

And that equals "Crash No. 2."

And Norman, Norris, and Oberon will be paid in full.

Along about then, President Bill, President-Presumptive Al Gore, and I will come out of hiding from the revolutionary mobs. We'll announce that there'll soon be a new kind of dollar. And the currency will be absolutely stable because it'll be backed by diamonique and cubic zircona jewelry.

Then I'll deliver the coup. And along with it the election to Al Gore. I'll announce that, when the new money is issued, all existing debts will be wiped out—except a few things like trial lawyers' bills.

The exceptions are necessary because some old-fashioned standards must be maintained. A few fat cats will be hurt by this little maneuver of mine, but most people will be so grateful when they suddenly own their houses and their SUVs free and clear. The country will recover quickly, and Bill, Al, and I will be bigger than NASCAR.

Oh, I know, our trading partners, overseas investors, and anybody who owns dollar-denominated assets will be slaughtered.

When I ran the whole scenario by Norris and Norman, he mentioned reading that Charles de Gaulle said, "Serious countries don't hyperinflate."

So what? I said. Charles de Gaulle was a foreigner. We might just as well worry about winning a popularity contest with a bunch of Arabs.

Everything will begin to go down seconds after the start of Year 2000—there'll be an instant Y2K domino effect.

I'm going to be *seriously* famous.

After President Bill, and Al, and I have stepped in to save the world, I'm sure my old flame, Barbara Walters, will want me as a regular on *20/20*. And instead of always being on C-SPAN and all those dumb press shows that nobody ever watches, I might even get to be a fixture on *Geraldo* or *Studs*.

What's next? What will happen when the country gets back on its feet again? Surely President Al will help me transfer the Federal Reserve—lock, money stock, and pork barrel—onto the Internet.

And who better to do this? Al Gore invented the Net.

I'll be the first Virtual Fed Chairman. And by then I won't have any boring financial chores left to do. That's because I've already started steering all the free reserves in the banking system into "one-decision" investments.

I've picked several Internet companies, each with an imaginative desire to bring in a little real revenue someday, and I've chosen a couple of blue chips to add to the mix—Global Crossing and Enron. With the money rolling in, I'll be able to fill my days and nights expressing myself creatively. I mean, nobody cares to know how the Fed orchestrates the money supply, but lots of people will want to download MP3s with the sounds of Alan Greenspan playing big-band tenor sax.

No matter what happens, I will have lived a full life.

I'll tell you what they should put on my tombstone. It should say, "This Fed Chairman brought some Jazz to the Party. He was the first and only Central Banker born with a Neon Rising Sign."

January 31, 2006

Since none of my thoughtful predictions for the new millennium came true, I simply lost interest in this, my Dear Diary—and now I'm retiring from the Fed.

Okay, one final prediction: with our wonderfully strong stock market and real estate market supported by even more wonderfully inventive financial derivatives, our country has reached a permanent peak of prosperity. And who cares that we've picked up some debt? So here's my final declaration, a little poem to celebrate the situation:

> Our nation of debt mountaineers
> lives higher and higher each year.
> From those heights you and I
> will eat pie in the sky
> and dump all the mess in arrears.

14.

Creating Blended Mutations I

B lended mimicry in the form of specific parodies is self-evidently double-voiced, a mingling of parodist and parodee. Blended mutations are equally multistable, but the duality is not invariably apparent.

Parodic mutations tamper with the form and/or content of art, and such fiddling can be so subtle or so familiar that the multistability may be overlooked. For instance, hoaxes, fake versions of whatever they purport to be, are parodic mutations (unless the hoax is designed as the work of someone specific, in which case mimicry takes over). Hoaxes, once exposed, can blossom, for those willing to perceive them fully, into parodic creations with a continuing double life as something both artistic and existing within an imaginative frame and also as something fake, hence *real*. But many of us simply assume that their exposure is all that matters about hoaxes rather than realizing that these strange objects offer a continuing opportunity to experience an art-vs.-life illusionistic duality.

Many authorities recognize that hoaxes are parodies, but other varieties of parodic mutation have gone thoroughly unnoticed as such. As I've mentioned, works of fiction uneasily steered by confusing or unreliable narration feature all manner of multistable possibilities, depending on who or what is to be believed. This sort of art amounts to parodic mutation in all its modernist or postmodernist glory, but nowhere to be found are experts who point to the obvious multistable connection between this multivoiced narrational artiness and, say, plain vanilla parodic mimicry.

All these matters are neither here nor there, because this sort of high-end parodic prose is not the focus of this volume. Rather, as I have explained, the next three chapters will cover low-end parodic mutations, the genre I have called "general parody spoofs."

Remember, these parodic spoofs are comic works of fiction, typically in the form of mock essays, mock news stories, and other varieties of faux fiction and nonfiction. Historically, as I've indicated, this kind of parody has not been recognized as a separate category or given a name of its own, because these works have been lumped together by definition-bearers with specific parodies, which, of course, mimic *real* external targets.

I've also noted that the latter, however brilliant, are dismissed by some experts as unoriginal, copycat art, which is a judgment that I believe is both stupid and unfair. But, at the risk of belaboring this point, it's a massive factual error to apply the copycat label to general parody spoofs, which simply play with the components of their chosen genre or mode—the prerogative of any artist—and generally depend not a whit on specific external models.

Mimicry, for all the controversy associated with it, conveys instant multistability wherever it appears. A general parody spoof, unassisted by mimicry or by the instant doubling of parodic binding, must create internal divisions to achieve multistability. Failing that, the work simply becomes a comic essay with, potentially, varying bits of parodic filigree.

As a rough rule of thumb, successful general parody spoofs generate multistability by adapting a hoaxy or semi-hoaxy approach to the material. Also the parodist may toss in (or depend solely upon) an unreliable or semi-unreliable narrative format. General parody spoofs, in short, are not exactly what they purport to be, and this major facet of parodic spoofs is usually easy to discern. As a result, the illusionistic double-sidedness of these spoofs remains accessible for those willing to switch their perceptual gears back and forth.

Additionally, general parody spoofs actually tend to be doubly hoaxy because, as I've just noted, they are seldom recognized as being any different from their mimicry-laden specific parody relations. This disguise-in-plain-sight remains both effective and universally undetected.

An excellent and quick way to understand how blended parodic mutations operate as illusionistic art is to compare such works with one of their very near-relations from the realm of illusionistic mechanical devices. Here I'm referring to an instrument called a taleidoscope, which—unlike its nonidentical twin, a kaleidoscope—does not utilize bits of colored glass to achieve its shifting effects. Rather, a taleidoscope looks out on the real world and reshapes that world with a distorting lens and a three-sided mirror:

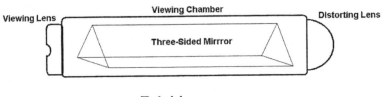

Taleidoscope

Parodic writing cannot compete with taleidoscopes in producing a wild multiplicity of mutating configurations, but the multistable principle governing each is entirely the same.

In my example below, shrinks, therapy, addiction-treating rehab clinics, and unscrupulous PR are canvassed with solemn approval, but my distaste for these *institutions* is unremittingly apparent. What sets the parody apart from mere simple irony (which is certainly present) is its hoaxy duality. The spoof features two faux documents— a spurious credo is embedded in a bogus press release.

Parody Work Sheet

TITLE

> "The CRI Credo"

VARIATIONS

Bangs:	Binds:	Blends:
Yes ~~No~~	Yes ~~No~~	Yes ~~No~~
Major ~~Minor~~	Major ~~Minor~~	Major ~~Minor~~

ITERATIVE DETAILS

STYLISTIC / NARRATIONAL CONTRASTS

> This is a satire that does not need to exaggerate its real world targets to skewer them: except for differences in jargon, the sleazy hucksterism of the framing Wall Street PR release differs little from its embedded "Recovery Movement" credo.

FORMAL / STRUCTURAL CONTRASTS

> The invasion of the for-profit "Caring Industry" into the realm of human misery and the for-profits' attempts to co-opt 12-step programs, genuinely altruistic movements, are self-contradictory, real life instances of bunched or branched parodic binding.

OTHER CONTRASTS

> This little parody, with its mock PR release and mock "Recovery" document is a typical example of the *trompe l'oeil* nature of many general parody spoofs--they appear to mimic specific "originals," but they are, in fact, original works in their own right.

COMMENTS

> As a satire, this blended parodic mutation contains a few gags, but it mostly stays on the attack.

<u>THE CRI CREDO</u>

In which it is learned that a Network of Individuals and Corporations, including Hospital Management Companies and Significant Others, have joined hands in order to free us Little People from our chains.

The important recent Labors of this Task Force have been compiled in the following passages of Scriptural Boilerplate.

The material has been the formatted for the PR Wire. But the text will soon be available, bound in Burgundy Leatherette by Hazel™, at greeting card kiosks in shopping malls everywhere.

For Immediate Release
Contact: Ms. Oprah Jessy Donahue, Honorary Chair

NEW CODEPENDENCY CREED BOOSTS SHARES, SHARING
LOS ANGELES [of course]—A Council equal in importance to those convened by the Chairpersons of the early Christian church (and similar in purpose to other nondenominational celebrations of a "Higher Power," in all lands and in terms of You-Name-It) agreed today upon the wording of a Document that is expected to "share equal billing as a Lifestyle Resource with *The Bible, The Upanishads,* and the Richard Simmons' workout videos," according to Ms. Oprah Jessy Donahue, Honorary Chair of Codependent Relationships International (CRI), the host organization.

CRI is a for-profit association corporately underwritten by Community Addictive Services Hospitals (OTC Symbol: CASH) and by the Kleenex Division of Kimberly-Clark (NYSE Symbol: KMB), which generously underwrote the Council's Work and the promotional fees paid to its participants, Ms. Donahue said.

This Monumental Project, despite its cost, is not expected to have a negative effect upon the share prices of the public companies that have served as its "Angels." Ms. Donahue also observed. "Quite the reverse," she said. "Good Things happen to the Earnings of Good People."

The Council's Interdenominational roster of stars comprised "the Biggest-of-Big Names—like Leo Buscaglia, Melody Beattie, and, of course, the Great John Bradshaw," said Ms. Donahue.

In many cases, however, the famous "Mentors" could not spare time from their saintly rounds of taping sessions, writing projects, and $100-per-ticket seminars in selected public amphitheaters, in which case they sent Surrogates, or "Mentees," and in some instances "Herbal Teas," according to Ms. Donahue.

John Bradshaw, for instance, could not attend because he was preparing for "the Cincinnati Series." So he substituted Terry Bradshaw, former quarterback of the Pittsburgh Steelers, who is now in the National Football League Hall of Fame,

Ms. Donahue said. "I was a little worried in this case," she added, "but, when things got tough and Terry was tested, he passed.

"The 'Game Plan' that finally emerged," she added, "reflected days of cross-talk, thousands of billable hours, and Oceans of Love. The sessions were typified by anti-denial and self-denial."

Ms. Donahue reminisced, "There were drafts and counter-drafts, and we couldn't ever figure out how to turn down the air-conditioning,"

"The Credo," she said, "which is to be worn like a large medical I.D. or a small 'teddy,' may be ordered in a limited and numbered edition in see-through Cubic Silkona™ from the Franklin Mint.

"We focus-grouped our way past a number of title options for the Document," Ms. Donahue said. "We tested everything from 'CRI-ME-A-RIVER' TO 'CRI-OGENICS,'" she added, "but we decided that the way to go was the Simple-and-Timeless Route with this, Our Declaration of Codependence."

THE CRI CREDO

WE ARE MEMBERS OF CODEPENDENT RELATIONSHIPS INTERNATIONAL (CRI).

WE ARE ADULT CHILDREN, THE INEVITABLE PRODUCT OF A SKEIN OF ADDICTIONS TRACEABLE IN OUR FAMILIES TO AT LEAST THE STONE AGE, AND, OWING TO THE GEOMETRIC MATHEMATICS OF GENEALOGY, PART OF A WEB THAT NABS *YOU* AND YOUR POCKETBOOK TOO.

OUR DISEASE IS CODEPENDENCY, WHICH MAY BE DEFINED AS (A) "ACTIVELY TRYING TO EXERCISE CONTROL"; OR AS (B) "PASSIVELY NOT TRYING TO EXERCISE CONTROL."

OUR DISEASE IS OMNIPRESENT. IT IS, FOR INSTANCE, THE KEY TO THE "EATING DISORDER" OF THE LATE-MAHATMA GANDHI, AND IT IS THE EXPLANATION FOR THE BOSTON RED SOX BASEBALL TEAMS' FORMER, ALMOST CENTURY-LONG, TENDENCY TO CHOKE.

OUR DISEASE IS UNSPARING. JESUS CHRIST WAS ABUSED AND VICTIMIZED; MOSES AND MOHAMMED WERE CONTROL FREAKS; BUDDHA WAS NUMBED OUT; AND CONFUCIUS WAS A PEOPLE PLEASER.

THEY WERE ALL "ADDICTED" TO ONE THING OR ANOTHER, WHICH MEANS THAT THEY WERE CODEPENDENT AS WELL, BECAUSE CODEPENDENCY IS THE INTERCHANGEABLE FLIP SIDE OF ADDICTION, PART OF A DOUBLE-EDGED "COSMIC GOTCHA."

LIKE US, JESUS AND THE OTHER GODHEADS WOULD HAVE BENEFITED FROM ADMISSION TO AT LEAST FOUR WEEKS OF

FOR-PROFIT HOSPITALIZATION (COSTS IN THE REASONABLE 25,000- TO 35,000-DOLLAR RANGE). ALL OF US WHO HAVE THE MONEY OR THE NECESSARY INSURANCE NEED TO TAKE THIS STEP (NO TWELVE-STEP PUN INTENDED).

OR WE CAN CHOOSE TO JOIN WITH OUR HIGHER POWERS IN INTENSIVE OUTPATIENT COUNSELING PROGRAMS (AT A PRICE IN THE MORE AFFORDABLE SPECTRUM OF 10,000 TO 20,000 DOLLARS).

DURING THIS TIME WE EXPECT TO BE ENJOINED, BY ALL MEANS SHORT OF VIOLENCE, TO ENTER AN APPROPRIATE NOT-FOR-PROFIT TWELVE-STEP PROGRAM (DONATIONS VOLUNTARY).

IT IS WITH THIS GROUP THAT THE BULK OF THE LONG-TERM CARE WILL BE PROVIDED, AND TO THEM THE RESPONSIBILITY FOR THE OUTCOME WILL BE SHIFTED.

UPON ENTERING A PROGRAM, WE MUST ALL BEGIN "RECOVERY," WHICH, DEPENDING UPON OUR KARMIC CIRCUMSTANCES, LASTS AT LEAST ONE LIFETIME AND WHICH INVOLVES WEEKLY OUTPATIENT COUNSELING AND/OR GROUP THERAPY SESSIONS, AS WELL AS TWELVE-STEP MEETING ATTENDANCE (MANY TIMES A DAY IS BEST).

THIS IS THE VITAL NEW INGREDIENT IN RECOVERY: THERE SHOULD BE MAINTENANCE OF A BLUE CROSS-STYLE HEALTH PLAN OR A PLAN FUNDED BY STATES OR THE FEDERAL GOVERNMENT—WITH COVERAGE, IDEALLY, AS INCLUSIVE AS ALL OUTDOORS.

IF THE HEALTH INSURANCE PACKAGE FAILS TO ENCOMPASS MAINTENANCE, THEN VISA OR MASTERCARD CHARGES MAY BE SUBSTITUTED TO MEET THIS REQUIREMENT.

TO RECOVER, WE MUST ALL "WORK THE STEPS" AT OUR MEETINGS AND "STEP UP FOR THE WORKS" AT OUR COUNSELING CLINICS.

"SHARING" IS ONE OF THE MORE IMPORTANT OF THE RITES, RITUALS, OBLIGATIONS, DUTIES, AND BURDENS OF THE RELENTLESS NEW CULT THAT WE HAVE "GRATEFULLY" JOINED IN ORDER TO COMBAT OUR "ADDICTIVE BEHAVIOR IN ALL ITS CUNNING GUISES."

WHEN WE SHARE, WE ARE "TAKING CARE OF OURSELVES" AND "TURNING IT OVER" BECAUSE "WE'RE AS SICK AS OUR SECRETS."

THIS MEANS THAT WE MUST BE ETERNALLY READY IN MEETINGS AND GROUP THERAPY SESSIONS TO TAKE

EGREGIOUSLY EMBARRASSING CONFESSIONAL PURGES, DANGLING OUR EMOTIONAL EFFLUVIA BEFORE A GROUP OF STRANGERS AS MOTLEY AS THE RUSH-HOUR CROWD IN A CONVENIENCE STORE.

THIS, THOUGH, IS A SMALL PRICE TO PAY FOR ADMISSION TO THE PROGRAM'S *CLIQUES.*

WE ACTUALLY JOIN MANY CLIQUES, WHICH DWARF THE SOCIAL NETWORKING CAPABILITIES OF SUCH OLD-FASHIONED "GET-A-LIFE" RESOURCES AS THE FRED ASTAIRE AND ARTHUR MURRAY DANCE STUDIOS.

NOT ONLY ARE CODEPENDENT HOSPITAL GROUPS, COUNSELING PROGRAMS, TWELVE-STEP MEETINGS, BOOKSTORES, VIDEOS, AND OTHER APPURTENANCES, INCLUDING DECORATIVE RECOVERY *OBJETS* AVAILABLE SOMEWHERE CLOSE BY VIRTUALLY TWENTY-FOUR HOURS A DAY, BUT THERE ARE ALSO EVER-EXPANDING OPPORTUNITIES TO "SPECIALIZE."

IN ATTENDING THE MOST BASIC THERAPY GROUP OR MEETING, FOR INSTANCE, A NEWCOMER WILL GRAVITATE TOWARD ANY NUMBER OF CLIQUES THAT HAVE BEEN HELPFULLY IDENTIFIED BY CRI, OUR PARENT ORGANIZATION, THE CENTRAL FILES OF WHICH WILL SOON BE ABLE TO TRACK US ON "THE ROAD TO MAINTENANCE" AND TO PROVIDE, FOR A MODEST ANNUAL FEE, A HOST OF BOOKKEEPING SERVICES ASSOCIATED WITH OUR THERAPY.

DEPENDING UPON HIS OR HER NEEDS, VULNERABILITIES, OR AGGRESSIVE DESIGNS, THE CODEPENDENT CAN CHOOSE TO HOOK UP WITH PEERS IN SOME 476 CLIQUES, INCLUDING

- THE MANICS
- THE DEPRESSIVES
- THE SCHIZOS
- THE PARANOIDS
- THE NARCISSISTS
- THE BORDERLINES
- THE FULL-BORE PSYCHOS
- THE FULL-BORE BORES
- THE BLABBERS
- THE WHINERS
- THE WEEPERS
- THE DROOLERS
- THE PREDATORS

- THE LONELY-HEARTS
- THE SPONGERS
- THE JOB SEEKERS
- THE OUTCASTS
- THE NERDS
- THE MOONIES
- THE TREKKIES
- THE CREEPS
- THE DREGS
- *AND SO MANY MORE*

THESE CLIQUES ARE GROWING IN NUMBER EVERY DAY, BUT THEY ARE JUST THE TIP OF THE PROVERBIAL ICEBERG.

MEETINGS AND THERAPY SESSIONS ALSO FACILITATE "SPEAKER TRAINING" AS INTENSE AS THE MOST GUNG-HO DALE CARNEGIE COURSE, AND THE PACKAGE CAN BE CUSTOM-TAILORED IN AS MANY WAYS AS TOPPINGS MODIFY THE PRODUCTS AT "GOOD LORD, IT'S YOGURT" FRANCHISES.

THROUGH OUR NETWORK OF SUPPORT, WE CAN EXPECT TO ASSIMILATE THE "STRENGTH, HOPE, AND EXPERIENCE" THAT WILL ENABLE US TO "TAKE CARE OF OURSELVES" *VIA* OUR ROBOTIC, RED GUARD-STYLE SLOGANEERING THAT HELPS US "MAKE IT THROUGH THE NIGHT."

ULTIMATELY, WE WILL BE ABLE TO CHANNEL OUR ADDICTIVE BEHAVIOR TO SUPPORT THE ONLY TWO LONG-TERM "HEALTHY ADDICTIONS"—MEETINGS AND MAINTENANCE.

WITH THESE TWO BULWARKS TO SUPPORT US, WE CAN READILY FIND A RATIONALE FOR ABANDONING

BOOZE
DRUGS
FOOD
SEX
PETS
JOBS
RELATIONSHIPS
MARRIAGES
CHILDREN
OZONE
ZIP CODES

AND ANY OTHER PERSON, PLACE,
OR THING THAT, NOT BEING IN THE
PROGRAM, *IPSO FACTO*, POTENTIALLY
THREATENS OUR RECOVERY.

FOR FURTHER HELP OR INFORMATION, CALL CRI AT 1-900/
MEE-MEME. (THE CALLS ARE LOVINGLY BILLED AT NINE
DOLLARS PER MINUTE, AND, FOR AN ADDITIONAL CHARGE,
CRI CAN HOOK UP ANONYMOUS MEMBERS WHO WISH TO
SHARE LITE OR DARK SECRETS.)
KEEP CALLING BACK.

In summation, Ms. Donahue, who is also a Spokesperson for Community
Addictive Services Hospitals, noted that the CRI Credo is "just one instrument in
our Doctor's Bag."

She observed that, at the next council, CRI plans to launch its national
marketing plan for the twelve-volume *Encyclopedia of Addictions*, currently being
prepared by volunteers from the Staff of Community Addictive Services Hospitals.

"This is a Project," Ms. Donahue said, "that will nail thousands of addictive
categories from 'aardwolfs' to 'zymosis.'

"For instance," she said, "there's even going to be a listing for that tiny number
of Wall Street securities analysts addicted, somehow, to the belief that psychiatric
hospital management companies might be less than 20 percent per year earnings
growers in the decades ahead and might not, therefore, be the hottest of all 'buys'
for stock market investors.

"That viewpoint is patently sick," Ms. Donahue concluded.

"As long as The People are anxious to search for 'Toxic Parents' and 'The Child
Within,'" she said, "this will never be a Mature Industry."

15.

Creating Blended Mutations II

L ike most of my parodies, the next one was written in the Dark Ages before we could Twitter our way to piffling cosmic irrelevance or e-Harmonize a search in cyberspace for romantic partners linked to us through twenty-nine points of compatibility and future bones of contention. No, my parody is about old-fashioned, stumble-around, battle-of-the-sexes misery. It's just another general parody spoof.

I've already suggested that it's fair to say that the hoaxy, unreliable elements in such parodies are ironic, but I would maintain that much of what is defined as irony by literary gurus is a quality that emerges from an underlying bed of parody. In fact, I think parody underwrites much simple irony and virtually all complex and confusing irony.

Irony involves, in its simplest manifestations, a slightly dry contrast between appearance and reality, and if the irony remains simple, the appearance is exposed by the reality. If the irony is complex, there will be multiple appearances and multiple realities, which means that multistability is on hand—a presence that's always parodic.

Parody generally underpins or serves as the basis for ironic art, but the underlying parody is seldom explored for its dualistic potential because, for many readers (or audiences), the detection of irony is thought to be an end-in-itself. The discovery of irony is regarded as proof that the subject matter has been targeted by a fancy form of sarcasm and that the material should be understood as meaning something quite different from what it purports to disclose. But the audience or readership then usually shortchanges itself: the near-universal belief that the presence of simple irony produces a sort of aesthetic closure almost invariably shuts off the perception of multistable open-endedness afforded by the underlying parody.

For instance, as I've suggested, general parody spoofs tend to be artistic hoaxes—faux documents—and if the percipient permits, these have a double life as *both* a work of art and as something fake, meaning something *real*. However, if a reader or audience decides that the material has a single, ironic explanation, then the multistable possibilities will probably remain unexplored.

At the risk of annoying you with another chart, here is what I think are the multistable dynamics of hoaxes:

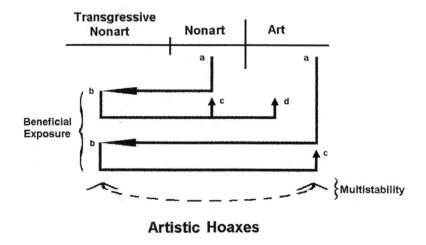

Artistic Hoaxes

At the outset, the hoaxer pretends that the work is (a) either a work of art or of nonart (such as nonfiction). Then (b), with detection by readers or audiences, the work is beneficially revealed as a hoax, at which point its double life can begin. Writing that was originally represented (a) as art can now be perceived as both (b) a hoax and (c) a work of art. Documents that purported to be (a) a work of nonart, such as journalism, can be perceived (b) as a hoax and (c) as still a work of journalism, or as (d) an artistic concoction, or as a combination of (b), (c), and (d).

Forgive this dose of theoretical blather, but I thought it was important for you to understand that even relatively mindless parody like the one below has a potential double life. Further, this is a state that can be achieved in your writing without the need to be obscure.

Parody Work Sheet

TITLE

> "Singled Out"

VARIATIONS

Bangs: Yes ~~No~~ Major ~~Minor~~	Binds: Yes ~~No~~ ~~Major~~ Minor	Blends: Yes ~~No~~ Major ~~Minor~~

ITERATIVE DETAILS

STYLISTIC / NARRATIONAL CONTRASTS

> This is a garden variety general parody spoof. The breezy narration, however, contrasts mightily with the comic dating wreckage that the piece chronicles.

FORMAL / STRUCTURAL CONTRASTS

> There are a series of little vignettes, each ending in bathetic futility, and each of these structural bangs is riddled with gag-based mini-explosions.

OTHER CONTRASTS

> There is a general absence of parodic binding, but, perhaps, the stretching of patient-to-therapist transference into a possible occasion for dating qualifies as bunched binding.

COMMENTS

> This little work of blended parodic mutation qualifies as light comedy, but it is interspersed with bits of satire and serious social commentary.

SINGLED OUT

What should a single male do in America?

Well, he can experiment with carbon monoxide. Or he can try the other stratagems proposed in *Final Exit*, which *was* available at all those finally-exited bookstores at "the Mall."

On the other hand, those single males who actually wish to have sticks and stones break their bones and to pursue other forms of prolonged suffering on this side of the River Sticks can do so by attempting to meet and to commune with a woman.

These are the Happenin' Singles Haunts in Anytown, USA.

Singles bars. This scene has been lovingly described as "The WASP Auschwitz," "Upchuck Alley," and "Granny's Last Stand."

You've got a real chance to "score" here if you're quick enough to abduct one of the near-comatose "addicts" for which singles bars are justifiably famous.

First, let her express herself by spewing stale smoke, stale rage, and stale beer; then move in with a hand truck.

Twelve-step programs. But why settle for a besotted corpse when you can become the "suffering servant" of a zoned-out zombie, your very own "recovering" addict?

"Thirteenth stepping," or sexual predation, has long been the hidden, meat-shop agenda of many twelve-step meetings. So move into this happy world of mood swings and insatiable demands.

Explore with your new partner that compelling combination of self-absorption and self-loathing that drove her to addiction in the first place. After all, what's wrong with old whines in new bottles?

Many singles, though, prefer simply to hang out in the "Recovery" section of local bookstores, hoping to be spotted and sniffed by another philodendron. There they can strike effective poses, knowing that bookstore neon will impart a dramatic, sheen-like cast to their eternally needy droolings.

The Politicos' Tavern. Here's your passport to hobnob with "groovy" local politicians and other hometown celebs.

There's lots of touchy-feely joviality in these places, along with an overwhelming downside. You see, an unattached single woman was last reported to have been seen on such premises in 1962, and she was spirited away by Vernon Presley in a metallic-blue UFO.

Singles night at various churches. What a nostalgic adventure you'll have.

First, a lovely meal consisting of plaster of Paris and cat hairs for which you'll have to listen to a religious harangue. This will remind you of those enthralling evenings you've spent huddled in Salvation Army shelters.

Next comes "The Impossible Dream," a quixotic quest in which you try to initiate an actual conversation with a member of the opposite sex. Try prying an unattractive, giggly airhead away from a gaggle of her peers to which she has attached herself with rock-climbing gear.

All this will recall the primordial dawn of your youth, those secure, joyous times you had in the eighth grade.

The church singles scene, by the way, is very competitive. To whip up interest, one brand-new group is reportedly on the verge of hiring a Christian dominatrix.

Evenings at the local university or trade school. Surely your town has at least one "Venus Fly Trap of Nowledge" that offers quasi-academic, maxi-trendo mini-courses at night.

The typical curriculum will include at least thirty-seven offerings devoted to "Financial Planning for the Inner Child" as well as a few offbeat courses, such as "Out-of-Body Experiences with Nachos" and "Dogs and Cats Who're Petted Too Much."

You'll have ample opportunity to deliver all your worldly goods to a commission-starved stockbroker masked as "Your Financial Codependent," and you'll learn that the Inner Child must be supplied with oxygen from an Inner Tube until such time as it can blossom as an independent Four-Ply Radial.

The odds on meeting a nice lady are statistically low, so don't expect much "action" to emerge from the classes. But the cleaning women are sometimes approachable and unattached.

Therapy. This is your last, best hope, one surefire way to defeat loneliness by "going against the flow" if you don't have a "liberal" mother or sister. But remember that dating the female therapist of your choice doesn't normally mean that you'll be able to take her out on the town for gala evenings.

But you can dream, can't you? Be sure to play an Enya tape, and sink into self-hypnosis or creative visualization to picture yourself and your beloved gobbling corndogs at the drive-in movie theater.

And it'll be a lot more fun than real life, because there's no actual performance to worry about (yours or the flick's), and the two of you will have the "virtual passion pit" all to yourselves.

Every once in a while, of course, you may hear about a patient who "made it" with his therapist. There was supposed to be, for instance, a "hot-ticket" lady shrink at Harvard who got kinky with her patient, Raoul.

But as a Raoul of thumb, the therapist probably won't leave her office with you. So just let your romantic self run wild at "her place." She'll come alive when you enter the room, and she'll jot down your pronouncements like an adoring groupie.

Go ahead and tell her your great secret—that you're the Man Himself, Adolf Hitler. Share with her, as only a lover can, your dreams of world domination and conquest.

After that, so what if she doesn't "come across" when you demand a little "transference."

So what, if all your efforts lead nowhere?

It shouldn't matter to an *über*-soul such as you.

Therapy, like dating, is a lot of sound and *führer*, signifying nothing.

16.

Creating Blended Mutations III

I confess that this, the final chapter on general parody spoofs, is somewhat anticlimactic. But spoofs, especially satirical spoofs, are very much at home with anticlimax, so my lapse is consistent with my subject matter.

Instead of promising you fame and a surefire way to get your parodies published and, better, actually perused by someone other than your mom, I'm going to discuss what to do if you've written a parody that's become dated while rejection letters have piled up over the years or while few people have visited your parody after you've lodged it on the Internet. On the Net, unfortunately, you cannot spring your parody on the unwary as if it were a wad of chewing gum on the sidewalk.

My truly anticlimactic suggestion is this: don't do anything. If the parodic spoof is funny, it will remain so even if parts of it contain material that no one recognizes or understands anymore.

The case in point is the example below—rather, the two versions of the example. Long ago I wrote a general parody spoof about "Whip" Farrago, a fictional member of the administration of Ronald Reagan and, not surprisingly, it became dated fairly quickly.

For no other reason than wanting to be "with it," I updated the parody years later, lodging Farrago in the service of George W. Bush. Even though the process of making the material appear somewhat timelier was relatively easy and even though I think I got off a few funny lines in the *new* parody, I still believe the original is a better, more unified piece. So, again, the moral is, if you're satisfied with your parody once it's finished, leave it alone, and someday it may fester into notoriety, dragging you along.

Whether or not I'm right about standing pat is a judgment I'll leave up to you. The Reagan era parody appears below and is followed by its successor. In the Bush era parody, I've emboldened the changes so that you can see what I mean about that this sort of thing being potentially easy to do (even if the changes aren't necessarily worthwhile).

My work sheet has stood the test of time better than the original parody. It functions well for both versions, so I didn't have to change it before or during my updating.

Parody Work Sheet
TITLE

> "Whipping History"

VARIATIONS

Bangs:	Binds:	Blends:
Yes ~~No~~	~~Yes~~ No	Yes ~~No~~
Major ~~Minor~~	~~Major~~ ~~Minor~~	Major ~~Minor~~

ITERATIVE DETAILS
STYLISTIC / NARRATIONAL CONTRASTS

The parody can pass either as a mock popular history essay or as a mock magazine feature story. The style is unburnished and semi-formal, the narrative generally chronological. Fortunately, all this is leavened by successive parodic bangs.

FORMAL / STRUCTURAL CONTRASTS

The text is full of allusions to real people and to real historical events and circumstances. An effort has been made to distort this material significantly so that those unfamiliar with the references will still recognize the presence of comic slings and arrows.

OTHER CONTRASTS

This is not a fancy parody, but it aims at some relatively fancy wordplay ("One man's media," "He treats a horse like a lady," "Oh Press, oppress him no more," etc.).

COMMENTS

Apart from the exaggerated historical material and the wordplay, this is a plain vanilla general parody spoof with few frills.

WHIPPING HISTORY I

One man's media is another man's *poisson* wrapper, as the saying goes. For Republicans, it's often the wrapper.

Did you know that the press, in its overarching hatred of Ronald Reagan's presidency, perpetrated a cosmic sin of omission?

As in *Pravda* during its heyday, or as in any issue of *Town and Country* or *Laxative Industry Trends*, the journalistic overlords can simply exorcise great swaths of reality simply by purging or ignoring them.

In other words, if the press doesn't cover your little world, you're as good as dead because, as Socrates should have said, "The unexamined life isn't worth living—unless there's PR."

Case in point: the remarkable career of Melville "Whip" Farrago.

You've never heard of him, have you?

He was with the Reagan administration from the beginning. He was appointed in 1981 to direct the activities of the President's Roundtable on Pesticides (PROP).

On the face of it, that sounds like awfully small beer, but the story acquires an altogether different gloss when overlaid against the disclosure that this three-member committee, which had been defunct since 1917, was revived to take the place eventually of the Department of the Interior.

After a transition period, Interior was going to be abolished in 1984, and all the land held by the government was going to be turned over to the National Association of Realtors, prior to being zoned commercial.

To get the ball rolling, Farrago's commission held a press conference and tried to put the word out on "the positive side of 'The DDT Story.'"

But nobody from the media showed up; there was no coverage at all.

This came as a great surprise to Farrago, because he'd been so very visible his entire life and because he seemed to be such an inviting target for the Insatiable Liberal Cuisinart.

Farrago had expected to be attacked from the get-go because he had no experience in government and because many thought of him as an uncontrollable wild man as well as a probable psychotic. On balance, Farrago's appointment smacked of cronyism.

He was all set to debunk this latter charge, had it arisen. "Ronnie and I aren't cronies," Farrago was prepared to exclaim. "We're just old pals."

Reagan and Farrago, of course, did go "way back" to the "Golden Age of Movies."

While Reagan was a resident "B-Keeper" (a stalwart of "B," or "second feature" pictures) on the Warner Brothers lot, Farrago was getting by with "Gentlemen's Cs" elsewhere, mostly by cranking out westerns and cracking his bullwhip for Moped Pictures, down Tijuana way.

Of Farrago's films, the movie critic Pauline Kael had this to say: "They're trash, hideous shimmering trash. That's why we love them so."

About his acting style and manner, on screen and off, another critic observed, "He treats a horse like a lady and a lady like a horse."

Washed up in movies, Farrago joined the professional wrestling circuit. Later he became an automobile pitchman on Los Angeles television.

Eventually he joined Reagan's inner circle along with other West Coast businessmen and cultural arbiters, such as Alfred Bloomingdale, Justin Dart, and Las Vegas comic genius Shecky Greene.

As a car peddler, Farrago continued with his wrestling and his patented whip cracking. He destroyed slow-selling automobiles both with his whip and with his bare hands in a series of fabulously successful Los Angeles television commercials.

On the basis of this return to the limelight, Farrago was appointed regent of the University System of California, and he founded a cult—some say a religion—of whip-wielding California car wreckers. An orgiastic mob of little old ladies in tennis shoes gradually formed and flocked to his banner.

This crazed group of aged *Bacchae* smashed hippie "love mobiles" and anything else sporting a psychedelic paint job. Farrago's critics demanded his arrest, but his movement waxed instead of waned.

Regent Farrago supported then-Governor Ronald Reagan's tough stance against troublemakers on California campuses. And in his commercials Farrago began destroying, with his teeth, books by suspect or particularly unkempt professors.

In Washington, Farrago continued this practice of what conservative columnist William Safire, in conversation, called "dentulous dismantling," but Safire, too, was part of the noncoverage cabal, and he never mentioned "Whip" Farrago in print or on the air.

The press simply ignored Farrago's existence. Worse, the media elite invented a totally fictional Interior Secretary and borrowed a name for him, James Watt, from the man who perfected the steam engine. If there ever was a liberal conspiracy, this was it.

Even Farrago's untimely death in 1983 went unreported. It occurred while he was gnawing his way through copies of a *Congressional Record* studded with remarks by Senator Edward M. Kennedy.

Sadly, Farrago expired before the press conference-*cum*-infomercial that might have returned him to visibility and launched his agenda at last.

He had planned an end-run around the working press by going directly to the people. To do that, he had purchased network airtime with private funds (supplied by Pakistani banking friends).

From the unreleased press kits and the scripted material that survives, it's clear that Farrago knew, in the biblical sense, the inner workings of Spectacle.

As a warmup, he planned to strip to the waist and dismember a lime-green Malibu. In the interests of sportsmanship, his inanimate antagonist was to have been thoroughly greased up with a coating of K-Y Jelly.

Then Farrago aimed to issue "the first of many" pro-DDT on-air information bulletins. It reads, "Here's excitement! Here's adventure! Here are swarming hordes of alien insect creatures with the power to destroy Civilization—and here's a tall, whip-cracking Westerner with the scientific formula for the only force in the Universe that can stop them!"

Ultimately, Farrago expected to announce an all-out assault on anti-DDT legislation via a new and private organization, Doers and Winners Enraged About Stupid Laws (DAWEASL). It was supposed to be funded by those tax monies originally earmarked for the Interior Department.

His scheme was nothing if not audacious.

The money would pass from Interior, which would also begin busily transferring public lands prior to becoming an empty shell, to its new parent, PROP (the President's Roundtable on Pesticides, remember).

From there the land would go to the realtors and the moola would have been passed on to Farrago's new, private organization, which would use the income to promote DDT.

Of course, Farrago never got to close any part of the deal. But his undelivered kickoff speech hasn't been lost to history. Like every perfect commercial message, it taps into something profound or universal. Among other declarations, he would have uttered a phrase that for all time captures perfectly the essence of that mystical marriage between politics and public money.

"That's the way the money goes," Farrago planned to conclude, "PROP goes DAWEASL."

For this explanatory nugget alone, he deserves to be remembered. Oh, Press, oppress him no more.

* * *

The newer parody appears below. You'll note that most of the changes in bold consist of scattered phrases that alter the timeline and/or the name of the president then in residence. Also, a lot of people in the first parody had died by the time of the second, and I indicate the passing of some. There are a few new gags in the Bush-era parody, but not that many. Ultimately, if you're determined to mess with your parody, you may find that it's a lot easier to modernize your kitchen or your face.

Whipping History II

One man's media is another man's *poisson* wrapper, as the saying goes. For Republicans, it's often the wrapper.

Did you know that the press, in its overarching hatred of George W. Bush's presidency, perpetrated a cosmic sin of omission?

As in *Pravda* during its heyday or as in any issue of *Town and Country* or *Laxative Industry Trends,* the journalistic overlords can simply exorcise great swaths of reality simply by purging them.

In other words, if the press doesn't cover your little world, you're as good as dead because, as Socrates should have said, "The unexamined life isn't worth living—unless there's PR."

Case in point is the remarkable career of Melville "Whip" Farrago.

You've never heard of him, have you?

He was with the Bush II administration from the beginning, a legacy from the Reagan era like Dick Cheney, Don Rumsfeld, and individually wrapped cheese slices. He was appointed in 2001 to direct the activities of the President's Roundtable on Pesticides (PROP).

On the face of it, that sounds like awfully small beer, but the story acquires an altogether different gloss when overlaid against the disclosure that this three-member committee, which had been defunct since 1917, was revived to take the place eventually of the Department of the Interior.

After a transition period, Interior was going to be abolished in 2004, and all the land held by the government was going to be turned over to the National Association of Realtors, prior to being zoned commercial.

To get the ball rolling, Farrago's commission held a press conference and tried to put the word out on "the positive side of 'The DDT Story.'"

But nobody from the media showed up; there was no coverage at all.

This came as a great surprise to Farrago, because he'd been so very visible his entire life and because he seemed to be such an inviting target for the Insatiable Liberal Cuisinart.

Farrago had expected to be attacked from the get-go, because he had no experience in government and because many thought of him as an uncontrollable wild man as well as a probable psychotic. On balance, Farrago's appointment smacked of cronyism.

He was all set to debunk this latter charge, had it arisen. **"President Bush and I aren't cronies,"** Farrago was prepared to respond. "We're just old pals."

Bush had even filmed a supportive clip that contained the following: "This charge of cronyism is bad for the country's War on Terror. It's diversionrary." The President concluded by patting Farrago on the back, saying, **"Whippie, you're doing a heckuva job."**

But, again, nothing happened. Nobody noticed even though Farrago was something of a Republican icon, his celebrity status traceable way back to the "Golden Age of Movies."

Back then Ronald Reagan was a resident "B-Keeper" (a stalwart of "B," or "second feature" pictures) on the Warner Brothers lot, and Farrago was getting by with "Gentlemen's Cs" elsewhere, mostly by cranking out westerns and cracking his bullwhip for Moped Pictures, down Tijuana way.

Of Farrago's films, **the late movie critic Pauline Kael** had this to say: "They're trash, hideous shimmering trash. That's why we love them so."

About his acting style and manner, on screen and off, another critic observed, "He treats a horse like a lady and a lady like a horse."

Washed up in movies, Farrago joined the professional wrestling circuit. Later he became an automobile pitchman on Los Angeles television.

Eventually he joined Reagan's inner circle along with other West Coast businessmen and cultural arbiters, such as Alfred Bloomingdale, Justin Dart, and Las Vegas comic genius, Shecky Greene.

As a car peddler, Farrago continued with his wrestling and his patented whip cracking. He destroyed slow-selling automobiles both with his whip and with his bare hands in a series of fabulously successful Los Angeles television commercials.

On the basis of this return to the limelight, Farrago was appointed a regent of the University System of California, and a cult—some say a religion—of whip-wielding California car wreckers. An orgiastic mob of little old ladies in tennis shoes gradually formed and flocked to his banner.

This crazed group of aged *Bacchae* smashed hippie "love mobiles" and anything else sporting a psychedelic paint job. Farrago's critics demanded his arrest, but his movement waxed instead of waned.

Regent Farrago supported then-Governor Ronald Reagan's tough stance against troublemakers on California campuses. And, in his commercials, Farrago began destroying, with his teeth, books by suspect or particularly unkempt professors.

In **Bush's** Washington, Farrago continued this practice of what **the late conservative columnist William Safire,** in conversation, called "dentulous dismantling," but Safire, too, was part of the noncoverage conspiracy, and he never mentioned "Whip" Farrago in print or on the air.

In fact, the press simply ignored Farrago's existence. If ever there was a liberal conspiracy, this was it.

Even Farrago's untimely death in 2003 went unreported. It occurred while he was gnawing his way through copies of a *Congressional Record* studded with remarks by **the late Senator Edward M. Kennedy.**

Sadly, Farrago expired before the press conference-*cum*-infomercial that might have returned him to visibility and launched his agenda at last.

He had planned an end-run around the working press by going directly to the people. To do that, he had purchased network airtime with private funds **(supplied by American Indian friends in the casino and gaming industry).**

From the unreleased press kits and the scripted material that survives, it's clear that Farrago knew, in the biblical sense, the inner workings of Spectacle.

As a warmup, he planned to strip to the waist and to dismember a lime-green Malibu. His inanimate antagonist, in the interests of sportsmanship, was to have been thoroughly greased up with a coating of K-Y Jelly.

Then Farrago planned to issue "the first of many" pro-DDT on-air information bulletins. It reads, "Here's excitement! Here's adventure! Here are swarming hordes of alien insect creatures with the power to destroy Civilization—and here's a tall, whip-cracking westerner with the scientific formula for the only force in the Universe that can stop them!"

Ultimately, Farrago expected to announce an all-out assault on anti-DDT legislation via a new and private organization, Doers and Winners Enraged About Stupid Laws (DAWEASL). It was supposed to be funded by those tax monies originally earmarked for the Interior Department.

His scheme was nothing if not audacious.

The money would pass from Interior, which would also begin busily transferring public lands prior to becoming an empty shell, to its new parent, PROP (the President's Roundtable on Pesticides, remember).

From there the land would go to the realtors and the moola would have been passed on to Farrago's new, private organization, which would use the income to promote DDT **and to squelch such sinful practices as stem cell research, the teaching of evolution, and gambling** *except* **on American Indian reservations.**

Of course, Farrago never got to close any part of the deal. But his undelivered kickoff speech hasn't been lost to history. Like every perfect commercial message, it taps into something profound or universal. Among other declarations, he would have uttered a phrase that for all time captures perfectly the essence of that mystical marriage between politics and public money. "That's the way the money goes," Farrago planned to conclude, "PROP goes DAWEASL."

For this explanatory nugget alone, he deserves to be remembered. Oh, Press, oppress him no more.

* * *

Okay, I would feel bad about ending this main part of the book if I didn't supply you with a snappy tip about how to induce someone to actually engage in a few Schnauzer-like sniffs of your parodies. In an age of cosmic clutter, both in publishing and on the Internet, there is one reliable tactic to draw on. You may want to commit an outrage so that your stuff will be noticed, and, in doing so, you will be performing what I call "Unabomber PR."

Ted Kaczynski, a.k.a. the Unabomber, in case you've forgotten, was living in a crumbling shack out west and subsisting on tree bark and Fruit Loops, but he got his incredibly boring 35,000-word manifesto published in major newspapers and read by thousands, maybe millions, because he mailed bombs both to people and to airlines over a twenty-year span, killing three and maiming twenty-three.

Although Kaczyski's victims can be written off as necessary sacrifices on the Altar of Art, I strongly urge you not to hurt anyone in your own PR campaign. Try to commit a *good* outrage because, as the beloved cartoonist and violent sexual predator Al Capp wrote, "Good is better than evil because it's nicer." And if you're nice about your outrage, you'll spend less time in the slammer or in the nut farm.

Here, for example, are a couple of relatively harmless, PR-generating outrages that a lone parodist might accomplish. First, you could set off a humongous stink bomb during a Kennedy Center Honors Night in Washington, D.C., on an occasion when some middlebrow weasel is receiving tributes that properly belong to you. Or you might carefully collect several gallons of your phlegm and dump the containers from a New York City roof or fire escape on a lunchtime gaggle of media employees of, say, *The Daily News* or one of the television networks. That done, both you and your targets will be assured of getting coverage.

As Socrates should have said, "The unexamined parody isn't worth writing—unless there's PR."

17.

BONUS: *How to Write a Modernist (Parodic) Poem*

If you aren't content to write funny and accessible parodies because you want to enter the realm of High Seriousness and/or because you want to lord your intellectual superiority over your fellow mammals, this final chapter is for you. The chapter deals with highly pretentious stuff, the parodic Big Time.

Fashions shift, especially in the arts, but for well over one hundred years, two closely linked aesthetic movements—modernism and postmodernism—have ruled the highest aeries from whence its practitioners, apologists, and devotees, in generally unchallenged splendor, have been able to sneer at the philistines and assorted peasantry down below. According to some authorities, modernism died out years ago, and certainly by the early 1970s, but I think modernist works in all the arts are still being churned out in quantities in this supposedly postmodern era.

Once upon an unenlightened time, poetry was relatively easy to understand. It usually rhymed, or at least it had a consistent rhythmic pattern, all of which seemed to be its inviolable essence. Nope. Modernism, as was its custom, turned all that upside down. A new formula for poetry emerged and included these particulars: rhythm wasn't necessary or even desirable anymore; rhyme was to be avoided, avoided, avoided; and intelligibility—forget it.

The same tidal wave hit the novel and other varieties of prose. The narrative point of view, once relatively lucid, became a confusing multiplicity and/or unreliable. Chronology became chopped liver, and the significance of it all slipped out the window and became difficult to lure back without an academic guidebook.

Music went atonal, and the visual arts were cubed.

And that was just the beginning.

Any work of art, as far as modernists were concerned had to be *new*, meaning a technical departure of one kind or another. Modernism and postmodernism have put an absolute premium on technical innovation.

As an unintended and unheralded result, the arts in the twentieth and twenty-first centuries have become encompassed by an Age of Parody, more so than in the Age of Swift and Pope, the previous, seemingly ultimate high-water mark. Because invention became virtually the sole determinant of artistic merit in modern times, parody became a secret, indispensable engine of change: there's simply no faster or more reliable way to reach an innovation-based Valhalla than banging, binding, and blending your way there.

However, very, very few modernist artists or their fans and interpreters admitted that modernism was essentially a parodic movement because parody was (and still is) universally defined as comic imitation, as trivial copycat art, the pariah in the artistic pantheon. So, rather than committing career suicide by admitting a massive dependence on the iterations of parody, modernists claimed that they were utilizing complex irony (or some such) rather than parody.

In fact, "parody" was seldom mentioned in modernist confines; its presence was vehemently denied when, as frequently happened, an uninitiated or unimpressed public claimed to spot a parodic presence in modernist art. And, as I've tried to explain in my other book on parody, the public was right, at least temporarily so: any shakeup of familiar artistic conventions tends to be an initially shocking phenomenon, and as a result, such jolts are a form of parodic banging.

However, once the new conventions have become familiar and *accepted*, the shock value may very well dissipate, a phenomenon that I call "transient parody." In such instances, the no-longer-jarring works may still be replete with banging, binding, and blending, but that must be determined on a case-by-case basis. At any rate, parody is almost inescapably the handmaiden of revolutionary change in the arts, even though it may fade (or lose its disorienting force) after the revolution is won.

Postmodernists, the artistic heirs of modernists, continue to worship innovation, but postmoderns are more anarchic and more playful than their parents. Because of this, postmodernists are less afraid to admit a parodic connection, and because of that, the importance and the omnipresence of "parody" is slowly being recognized.

Since modernist poetry is generally statelier than its postmodern counterparts (which can often seem indistinguishable from bang-ridden comic verse) and since I promised to suggest how you might write serious, stuffy poetry, I will confine my attention to modernism.

Such poetry, several generations after Ezra Pound and T. S. Eliot, still tends to be produced almost exclusively by banging, binding, and blending its components together. But this has been the *new normal* for more than ninety years, so few question the status quo or consider the sheer oddity of most modernist material that is sitting there on the page awaiting our rapt efforts to decode and interpret it.

As in decades past, to become a serious modernist poet, you have to learn how, in an affected manner, to foliate skeins of contrasts consisting of very fancy diction, slippery syntax, and roller-coaster semantics. And perhaps nowadays you might want to add a bit of rhyme because (a) intensely rhymed rap and hip-hop are eating the popularity of modernism and postmodernism alive and because (b) rhyme is so outrageously retro in a modernist context that, to some, it might qualify as a technical innovation.

I'm aware that slippery syntax and roller-coaster semantics may not be well-oiled ingredients in your Twitters or even in the dazzling mission statement that you are writing as the spokesperson for National Urea Industries, so I suggest you get started by modernistically overhauling one of those embarrassing LUV poems you once wrote to Snooki or to Joe Sixpack. From your archives, you will probably unearth a poem that is understandable, more or less, but that undesirable component can be sutured out of the picture.

Here is a typical starting point using a typically sappy example:

> I see ferns.
> The fronds are flutes
> A faun has died. I reach
> for you. We know
> we have unwound
> without a sound.
>
> Twenty years ago
> we passed in dreams
> beside the laurel
> and the mountain streams
> and failed. We failed
> to meet at all.
>
> The life we should have led
> played on around us
> in defeat
> just out of reach,
> just out of step,
> just off a beat.
>
> We walk today
> along your road
> around your father's lake
> where all those years ago
> I tried
> to find my only lover, you,
> before I died.

This poem is your raw material, as lame as it may be. Refashion it by collecting some expensive, forbidding, and polysyllabic words—snatched, perhaps, from a rhyming dictionary—that you can insert to make new sentences or phrases at the end of each stanza or section. In collecting these big words, the last thing you need to concern yourself with is their consistency, relevance, or possible meaning in terms of your existing poem.

Sample selection:

- *esplanade*: an open walkway, especially by the ocean
- *Weltschmerz*: overwhelming sadness about the nature of life
- *contranym*: a word that has different meanings that are contradictory
- *elide*: to omit, ignore, or eliminate

Now attach the words to the end of each section or stanza after using them to create sentences or phrases that, by themselves, make some semblance of sense but that manage, singly and in aggregate, to bollix up the relatively simple meaning of the poem.

Voilá, a genuine, not-quite-intelligible modernist poem (with the inserted lines emboldened):

I see ferns.
The fronds are flutes.
A faun has died. I reach
for you. We know
we have unwound
without a sound,
a tidal wave upon an esplanade.

Twenty years ago
we passed in dreams
beside the laurel
and the mountain streams
and failed. We failed
to meet at all
until our *Weltschmerz* free-for-all.

The life we should have led
played on around us
in defeat
just out of reach
just out of step
just off a beat
a swim in contranyms.

> We walk today
> along your road
> around your father's lake
> where all those years ago
> I tried
> to find my only lover, you,
> before I died
> **elided.**

Having done this overhauling a few times with your love poems or your odes to Burger King, you'll be ready to *go modernist* with a vengeance.

At this point, you won't need to generate a work sheet, *but* you can make very good use of the preliminary list that I recommended as a starting point for creating general parody spoofs. And add to that list a separate compendium of polysyllabic words (like the one above) to inject into your modernist outpouring at strategic weak and strong points.

My exemplary modernist poem, "Homage to Art Linkletter," was inspired by its title character, a radio and TV *personality* whose ingratiating, regular-guy-from-the-Heartland persona (but he was Canadian) was sufficiently nauseating to induce vomiting in a herd of healthy, placid cows. Arthur Gordon "Art" Linkletter (1912-2010) hosted very long-running radio shows that morphed eventually into longer running (or so it seemed) TV. These included *House Party* and *People Are Funny*, and his book, drawn from interviewing kiddies (*Kids Say the Darndest Things*), became a resounding best seller.

Apart from his intimacy with kitsch in all its forms, Linkletter became the focal point of my poem because of his punny name—the arts, rather, parts of them, do consist of linked letters, so Mr. L., in some of his incarnations in my little poem, embodies the arts. At other times in the poem, he is simply his supremely tasteless self, and I gravitated to this contrast: Tastelessness/ Food Imagery (the appearance of which in the poem, I felt, would be satisfyingly mystifying).

Then, for my other essential parodic contrasts, I decided to pit the actual, historical Art Linkletter against a purely fantastic version of the man. And for occasional specifics, I decided to contrast him at his corniest with an imaginary hip version of Mr. L. Finally, I decided that the mixture should include references to noxious TV shows and repulsive TV commercials contrasted with assorted odds and ends. Again, the latter were to be inserted to ensure that the poem would be modernistically impenetrable.

Thus I put together this list of my crucial contrasts, and these encompassed the projected guts of my poem and more.

MODERNIST PARODY	
TOPIC	CONTRAST
Art Linkletter	= ART
Tastelessness	Food Imagery
The Historical Art L.	A Fantasy Art L.
The Corny Art L.	A Jazzy, Hip Art L.
Noxious TV/TV Commercials	Weird Odds and Ends

With this list in hand, I went hunting for a collection of words (you should choose many for long poems, a few for brief ones) that are designed to intimidate and to impress most of those in the intended audience. I would note at this point that zillions of modernist poems have been written in slangy vernacular and without resorting to polysyllabics. But that's not important here—I'm suggesting a quick way to slam home a modernist concoction, and elitism via big words will help enormously.

In compiling a list of words, unlike the procedure in the exercise above, I needed to collect words that might have some relevance to the poem at hand. Of course, befuddling projected readers remained a paramount aim, but intimations that the poem is somehow organic and mysteriously unified definitely work in a modernist poem's favor.

My choice of diction:

- *legumes*: peas, beans, pods
- *decussate*: to form opposite pairs
- *phonemes*: distinct word sounds
- *reticulate*: to form networks
- *glottal stops*: a consonant sound formed by closing the glottis
- *interstices*: an opening, a gap
- *palinode*: a poem that retracts a previous poem
- *dithyramb*: passionate speech, esp. that of an ancient Greek dramatic chorus
- *pectate*: the salt of pectic acid
- *peristaltic waves*: involuntary muscle contractions that transport food and waste
- *portmanteau*: a large suitcase; also a portmanteau word means a new word coinage

And, this is the finished poem with the words above emboldened:

Homage to Art Linkletter
From his
X-life
and his **legumes**,
we
decussated
phonemes
("They spread, he said,
"like rotten nectarines
thrown up in a spasm at dessert").
He **reticulated**
the war years,
circumventing
glottal stops
and danced
on late night flights
the chicken and the bop.
Amid his airtime **interstices**,
I alone recall,
he recited
a **palinode** at the Embers,
a **dithyramb**
at the Club Damask.
His teeth scratched glass.
Our cult, Laura Kimberly-Clark,
Mircea Eliade, Et Ali, and Little Me
"took him up."
As predators, as poo-poo cushions,
we watched him eat a stork
upon a ladder.
Bad lyrics he expelled
like foreign matter.
When tiny germs attacked
his tummy's health,
I rejoined his "team." We met
the video folks halfway.
He spoke like Rabelais:
"Your little world is dead,
a bubbling **pectate**
struggling to be born."
Words flowed out
in **peristaltic waves**.

> The networks bought his act
> and lunched upon his **portmanteau**.
> Now and at the hour
> of our bad breath,
> he set us free
> from our excess
> acidity.
> He said the darndest things.
> His blood in lumps
> connected meatless symphonies.
> And we were calm
> and quite asleep.

Once you learn to fecundate poems like this one, you will become eligible to enter any of the thirty-four million and counting annual U.S. poetry contests; you can apply for any of the seventeen million-plus available awards and grants for *artistes*; or you can enter any of the twenty-five thousand MFA programs in the United States. In the latter, as at family reunions, you can meet women, men, or whatever lies between. With diligent application in this arena, you will be able to spend your life starving in near-total obscurity. But no matter. You'll be laboring in the artsy-fartsy Big Time.

And there's further consolation. With a little application, you can churn out reams of your own indecipherable material. And mysterious murk, after all, is timeless, compelling, and, dare I say it, immortal.

Well, as they say in the antique Italian trucking business, "That's a haul, folks."

Rob Chambers is one of thirty-five remaining natives of Atlanta. The millions of other residents are from Cincinnati, Ohio. Chambers has been a reporter and columnist for *The Atlanta Journal-Constitution*, and he has covered his locale for *The Economist*. Beginning his career as a college English teacher, Chambers quickly "sold out" for the thrill of manufacturing paper pads that soak up blood in supermarket meat trays. From there, he went on to the manufacture of plastic garbage bags and in a logical progression became a stockbroker. He bounced around the financial services industry in various incapacities for nearly two decades, mostly by way of ill-timed public presentations for the mutual fund industry. As a spokesman, he preached physical abstinence in the 1970s, material abstinence in the 1980s, and emotional absinthe in the 1990s. Somewhere along the way, Chambers also spent a couple of years in the public relations "game," capping his career at Hill and Knowlton by standing agape as his major client was hauled off to the federal pen.

At present, Chambers has returned to college teaching near Atlanta (at Kennesaw State University), where he hopes to induce the English Department to enhance its trendiness by adding Animal Rights and Animal Rhetoric as a new subdiscipline. Chambers has been writing parodies since spending time as a lad in a barnyard and being inspired by the smell of chickens. In fact, Chambers has written *Parody: The Art That Plays With Art* and *How to Write Parodies and Become Immortal* in preparation for his goal of swimming the English Channel costumed as a giant Blue Hen of Delaware. His other goals for the twenty-first century are to collect and pickle a bevy of Higgs Bosons and to locate and mutilate his inner child.

Made in the USA
Charleston, SC
22 March 2012